PASSING THE TORCH
The Way of the Avatar

"Illumine the common things and you will fill your skies with stars."

PASSING THE TORCH

THE WAY OF THE AVATAR

CAROL BELL KNIGHT

STILLPOINT PUBLISHING
WALPOLE, NEW HAMPSHIRE
1985

STILLPOINT EDITION

Copyright © 1981 by Carol Bell Knight
All rights reserved. No part of this book may be reproduced without written permission from the publisher, except by a reviewer who may quote brief passages or reproduce illustrations in a review; nor may any part of this book be reproduced, stored in a retrieval system, or transmitted in any form or by any means electronic, mechanical, photocopying, recording, or other, without written permission from the publisher.

This book is manufactured in the United States of America. It is designed by James F. Brisson, cover art by William Giese and published by Stillpoint Publishing, Box 640, Meetinghouse Road, Walpole, NH 03608.

Published simultaneously in Canada by
Fitzhenry & Whiteside Limited, Toronto.

Library of Congress Card Catalog Number: 81-82491
Carol Bell Knight
Passing the Torch
ISBN 0-913299-16-2
0 9 8 7 6 5 4 3 2

The hands that make a book are many.

I want to thank, first of all,
the teacher of the higher dimension who
worked with me on the contents,
Rabindra Matori.

Thanks also to beloved friends of
The Way, Lorin Roche, Victor Miller
and Elizabeth Ellis, who sat with me
through many hours of channelings.
To John and Susan Voohres and Victor Miller
for the first edition, and to Ed Kucera
who designed it.

And to Caroline Myss and Jim Young
of Stillpoint
for seeing the book as worthy of a
second edition,
my heartfelt thanks.

My joy is manifold in having the
artist, William Giese,
and designer, James Brisson,
contribute their inspirations to
the creation of the cover for the
second edition.

Carol Bell Knight

This book is dedicated
to the Glory of God
and
to the upliftment
of humanity.

Contents

Foreword

Prologue

POWER, LIGHT, AND ENERGY 1
  1 Power. The Golden Key 3
  2 The Inner Sun and the Torch 7
  3 The Light Absolute 12
  4 Spiritual Energy 17

Part Two
COMMUNICATION WITH OTHER DIMENSIONS 21
  5 Interdimensional Communication 22
  6 Receptivity to Higher Dimensions 30
  7 Immortality 35
  8 The Nature of Shambala 42

Part Three
MAKING IT WORK FOR INDIVIDUAL EVOLUTION 47
  9 Land — Water — Air 48
 10 Discipline, Order, and Use of Time 54
 11 Work 66
 12 The Inner Sanctuary 72
 13 A Safe Place in Spirit 77
 14 Silence, Solitude, and the Great Planetary
    Wind Chamber 85
 15 Destiny and Life Design 92
 16 Ultimate Individuality 99

Part Four
PASSING THE TORCH 105
 17 Preparation for the New World 106
 18 Responsibility of the Individual in
    Prevailing World Conditions 115

THE WAY OF THE AVATAR 119

Appendix-Summary 125

*"And look that nothing remain
in thy working mind but a naked intent stretching
unto God — not clothed in any special
thought of God in Himself or any of His works,
but only that He is as He is . . .
He asks no help but only thyself."*

Foreword

In a world in which we sometimes imagine ourselves as small observers lost upon the fringes of large events, we long for a message from a greater intelligence than our own, that the struggle upon this earth has a happy ending.

The Way of the Avatar reaffirms a design in the universe but hastens to establish that each of us must fulfill this design in our own lives. While there is comfort in knowing that we can get there from here, we are again reminded that the map is not the journey.

We are asked by the author to transform the events of our lives inwardly into a message that was whispered to Odysseus ages ago. Like that ancient wanderer, we seek our spiritual home. While its easy access eludes us, we can transmute denial into acceptance if we will persist in becoming something more tomorrow than we are today.

There is great power contained within the pages of this book. It is not a description or story of the accomplishments of someone more gifted than the reader — it is an invitation extended to each reader to pursue the structure and discipline necessary to accomplish intellectual, psychological, and spiritual perfection. This is called human evolution — the way of the avatar.

For many readers, avatar may be a new word. It means a bearer of good news, a teacher of the highest truths. Western man is only now in the process of recognizing the concept of avatar, since it is a term far more familiar to the Eastern intellect. And yet, any Western person who has been even slightly influenced by Christ, Mohammed, Zoroaster, or Buddha has indeed felt the impact of the avatar consciousness, for they are all avatars.

In this magnificent text, Carol Bell Knight presents the wisdom and guidance from the fourth-dimensional avatar, Rabindra Matori. This material focuses on that part of the human experience each of us struggles with every day of our lives. For example, in Chapter 1, Rabindra Matori presents his thoughts on the true nature of power, drawing the attention of the reader away from the materialistic power that seduces us, and offers insights into the level of power that silences our human fears and insecurities. Power of this capacity is drawn from the knowledge of the order and purpose of life. Since human history has been recorded, indeed from the epic time of Odysseus, it was those who knew and could teach this level of power that men turned to for assistance.

No one is removed from the quest for truth. *The Way of the Avatar* is a text of instructions which incorporates profound wisdom with contemporary consciousness and provides the enabling energy for any serious student to become an avatar. Carol Bell Knight and her teacher have given a great gift, worthy of careful study, to mankind.

Bill D. Schul, Ph.D.

Prologue

I come to bring not soft words but the lash of the reality of the power of the unit that you (the channel) have brought together. The teachers are working with units now. A unit consists of two, four, or eight people, and multiples of four, brought together for a common cause.

You have just begun to realize your power to bring about a common cause, but have you realized your power to connect with a duplicate of this unit on a higher level, an octave up? For there are four, eight, sixteen, and twenty-four powers and presences with whom you can link, if you will attend to your duties.

What are your duties? First, you have a duty to maintain system and order, moment by moment, in the use of your mind, the mind that is now a common mind among you. You have a duty to hold fast to clarity of perception, the realization that not within any other author's writings will your writings be found, but in your own being and in connecting with those who wish to work with you.

The cause that you are presently engaged in is miniscule compared to the one that will be presented to you in time to come — if that which you have set before you to do is accomplished in a minimum of time with a maximum of creativity.

The world about you is destitute. Where you are now is a profoundly quiet space, but you know what you left. You know what the world that you left consists of. You have seen it with your eyes, heard it with your ears, watched the glowing tube bring forth the message of disaster in one part of the world and another. You know that there is no end to the number of crises that must be faced daily by the elder members of the race to keep the planetary action in motion.

This has to do with salvation. Yes, I chose the word "salvation" carefully — for it is the salvation of humanity with which we are concerned. Perhaps you wonder how you in your trivial way can make any kind of difference. Perhaps you can't. Perhaps you can. There are those among us, in this other dimension, who feel that you can, and who are watching with interest the degree to which you put your shoulders to the wheel, the degree to which you scatter the negativity of your own being and bring forth the Power.

How do you think, really, that a lord is made? A lord is made from a master. A master is made from a teacher. A teacher is made from a disciple. A disciple is made from an aspirant. An aspirant is made from an unknowing one who first gets a glimpse that there is potential within his being, something other than going round and round on the wheel of misfortune.

Lords must watch for potential masters. Masters must watch for potential disciples. Disciples must watch for potential aspirants. Disciples must be teachers; teachers must be disciples. It is all interrelated.

Rabindra Matori
Mount Holly, Utah
July 21, 1978

Part One
Power, Light and Energy

Chapter One
Power. The Golden Key

We will first consider the concept of power.

You cannot work the miracles of a giant nourished only with the food of a babe. You must begin to realize the dimensions of your own power. This is the Golden Key to spiritual evolution — knowledge of Who you are, of your own power.

Power is achieved through total realization of your oneness with the universe. As long as you separate yourself from Universal Power, you will receive only the fruits of the separation. You will receive only half or less than half of what you deserve.

Dwell now on power — power through knowing, power through kindness, power through strength, power through determination. Allow no backward look to hold you from your course. When you are given an instruction from your higher mind or from your inner teacher, obey it.

Invoke the power of Christ in every moment of your life. Invoke the power of Universal Truth upon everyone connected with you.

The first expression of your power must be over your own being, that you allow no thought, no word, no deed to be less than a reflection of your pure divine nature. From you the way opens up for those near you to experience the conscious recognition of the Light.

Pass courageously through the fires of the burning ground. All lower aspects, which came from the process of Earth birth, must fall away. Those events through which you moved to arrive at the present state of your being are dead. Why, then, should you reflect now upon any limitations of your past?

Would you bury a corpse, then dig it up and say, "I will live with this corpse because it was once me?" No. Then do not bring up the corpse of the past and make it a part of today. This letting go is partly what the Lord Christ meant when He said, "Let the dead bury the dead." Let old conditions and old habits be buried by themselves.

You have around you now, in the dimension of light, power inconceivable to you in your ordinary state. Powers of light are working within you because they see within you great potential for bringing forth one aspect of the Word and the Truth of God. If you were to have the veil lifted from your blind eyes and see even for a moment the light of the powers that work with you, through you, and around you, you would be instantly transported into your divine state. For you would have no choice but to be the light reflecting the Light as these powers are. But the veil is there for your protection until you have reached an evolutionary point where you can handle the added stimulation.

You can remove the veil from your eyes through prayer, decree, meditation, and dedication. Your every moment must be alert, for when you slip into the hypnotic state you turn your back upon the powers that work with you. Would you turn your back upon the Power of God?

It is time now for alignment and integration. There is no time to lose, for humanity is in a hazardous position. Every appointee who has chosen to work in the name of God to unfold the plan of the Christ power upon Earth is called to perform his role to perfection. Throughout the domain of Earth the call has been put forth, "Come, step lively upon the path of light, that you may contribute to that greater light which calls all people to the Infinite One."

The great temptation is at the door knocking. The tempter is giving all power and effort in the realm of darkness to delay the coming of light. Be not taken in. Hold your light, keep your power, use your knowledge.

Another expression of your power is over your own area of influence. No one can come into your orbit except by your permission. When you accept less than perfection from anyone in your orbit, you are expecting less than perfection from yourself. Once you have given permission for another to come into your orbit, you must exert power over the connection and require the person, while in your orbit, to live according to your divine awareness. Thus you draw that person up to his own divine awareness. Yet this must be a silent measure. It cannot be bombastically spoken or harshly used as a sword against the person.

It is within your power to create every single individual within your environment to be what you choose him to be while he is with you. Think of all those connected with you in your personal life, in your business life, in your spiritual life. One by one declare that in your world they will reflect your power, thus increasing their own power. This is a blessing to them. But if you reduce your power and go to their station, you do no favor to yourself or them.

When you consider the power that has been given to you by the nature of your own evolution, you will realize that you are beyond the realm of ordinary man. You have risen into a new domain. Establish and express your special power within that new domain.

You have been given the Golden Key — awareness of your own power. This awareness can be developed by focused attention and concentration, as will be explained later. Use it wisely, and those powers will continue to be with you. This matter is most serious, and while you are asked to keep your humor and your joy, and never to lose your passion for living the fullness of life, you are also asked to be serious about your responsibilities in working with the plan of light and with the powers who work with you.

Chapter Two
The Inner Sun and the Torch

The counterpart of the sun in the sky is the Sun in the inner awareness of each individual. The spiritual Light is that inner Light. In every single human being who is born into physical manifestation there is placed a spiritual Sun.

Man's whole pursuit throughout his life is to seek that Sun, but he knows it not, so instead he lives in darkness. Let those who would walk upon the path of light, who would share the glory of the radiant presence of their own inner Light, first know that inner Light through meditation, through realization, through focused attention. Let them first show that inner Light by turning to it with deliberate design, to bring it forth into daily activity. The process is aided by humbling one's self, turning one's face to the Earth and then raising it to the sky, and saying, "Let the light of the sky that penetrates the Earth penetrate my mind, body, and spirit, that I may know the true reality of the inner Light, the spiritual Light."

All this really means is that the power you desire to be generated in yourself now is the power of the great Sun within your inner being. The power of the great Light, the inner Sun, when recognized, manifests in a form far more powerful and dynamic than the sun that you see in the heavens on the brightest day.

To go into the reality of the inner Sun, the spiritual Light, is to focus directed mental energy to a pinpoint of light and then to expand that light until it encompasses your whole being. Then the light becomes your being, and you become the spiritual Light, and there is no separation of the two.

The spiritual Light, thus recognized and elevated out of darkness, then becomes a radiant beam of light which goes forth as rays of divine, cosmic, illuminated energy. And with one thought that beam of light can, through the multiplicity of its rays, reach the consciousnesses of many who are ready to receive.

Unless that spiritual Light is manifested in one individual, it cannot be manifested and realized in other individuals who have no idea of its potential within them. Servers are called through realization of the spiritual Light and Power. (See Part Four, "Passing the Torch.")

Man is born into darkness. Does he not enter the tomb as he makes his exit out of the land of immortal Light into the womb? In the material world he resides in darkness for the prescribed period of time, according to the nature of the soul being born. Residing in darkness, he forgets. He becomes oblivious to the inner Light. Then comes the long process of returning to that Light and to that land of immortal Light.

The world of humanity is but a way station designed to give multitudes of evolving souls the realization of the contrast between darkness and light. It is a particular human characteristic that once an evolving soul becomes immersed in darkness, it rarely realizes, even for a moment, that the Light exists and that without the Light it would suffocate. Without the Light not even the next breath could be taken. It is not the air that provides the breath, it is the spiritual Light that provides the breath.

Angelic beings work diligently through all of the processes that relate to incarnating entities. Not one entity is born into physical embodiment who is not watched over from the angelic realms. To the best of their ability, angels disperse quantities of light to go with each soul. Yet as the soul enters the "tomb," it loses even the Light that has been dispersed to it. And it must begin at the point of birth the long process of going back to the realization of the dynamic power of the Light.

Now you will see that the nature of your work is to activate within every soul who crosses your threshold, who casts a glance upon you, his inner Light. That is the work of the teachers, of the angelic hosts, and of you who are here to activate the inner Light within all humanity.

Dwell upon these thoughts. There is no other way to return to the Godhead other than through the Light. Spiritual Light must be activated to enable return to the Godhead.

Thus you who have awareness are placed in a unique position. First activate your own spiritual

Light and then hand it as a candle, a flame, a torch, a beacon, to others. *That is the work.* Whatever else you do is secondary.

Will your words upon paper carry the Light? If they will, then they will stand the test of time. Will your scientific explorations carry the Light? Then they will stand the test of time. Will your songs, your compositions, carry the Light? If they will, then they will stand the test of time. Will your spoken words carry the Light? If they will, then they will stand the test of time. The test of time is this: that you still bear the Light as a torchbearer, though you have come from your own land of immortal Light into a land that appears to be in darkness much of the time.

You will carry the Light high, and when you return to the land of immortal Light, you will have left sparks, pinpoints of light, throughout the world wherever you have trod. Picture your every footstep upon the Earth leaving streams of light. Then you will see the nature of the plan of the elder ones, who sent forth those many volunteers of light to penetrate the darkness of Earth.

Remember the streams of light. Like the winged Pegasus, who goes across the sky leaving streaks of light, you walk upon the Earth, bound indeed by gravity, but leaving with your footprints streams of light. Let every move of your hand be a move of light. Let every thought of your mind be a thought of light. Let your constant utterance be, "Light, Light, more Light." And you will see, round and about you, many things fall away, which are the residue of the old ways of this and previous lives.

"Light, Light, more Light" will turn events your

way. You need no other mantra now, you need no other sound. You need no other decree, you need no other proclamation. Light is the one. Light.

Chapter Three
The Light Absolute

The awareness of the inner Sun, that Light within and its accompanying power, leads the student to the next threshold, the Light Absolute.

The Light Absolute exists in potential within the field of influence (the aura) of each individual. In that light there is no darkness, no illusion, no confusion, no delay. It is Pure Consciousness.

Having used the Golden Key to develop power, you are now a power in the Light. You attune in the depths of your being to realms where the Light Absolute is ever-present. You move into those realms. You center in a state of conviction of your own power within those realms. You draw the Light Absolute around you; you infuse every atom of your being with the Light Absolute, and you then walk, move, and have your being in that Light Absolute.

Once this degree of consciousness has been achieved, no matter what comes from the world about you, you will, by the power of the Light Absolute, place into dissolution anything that is not of the Light Absolute.

Key words are: infusion, correlation, assimilation, escalation, infiltration, and ingestion. Dwell upon these words individually. Select one word at a time, discover and discern its meaning, then dwell upon the assimilation, the ingestion, the infusion, of that word within your own being. Dwell upon your power to escalate the Light. There is no time now, none, to wait. Now is the hour. Now is the time that has been predicted in many scriptures since the early days of the Great Pyramid. The time is now. The turn of the century, which is upon you, will certainly bring about a vast change in individuals.

You are among the forerunners. Your responsibilities grow greater each day. To waste one day is an error. If you find that you have wasted a day, make up for that waste through intensification of the Light in the next day.

Be conscious every single moment of your self as a center of spiritual Light and Power. Let not one second pass through your experience in each new day that is not infused and accelerated by the presence of the Light Absolute. We come from the Sun and return ultimately to the Source, but between these points of destination, where goeth thou? Do you go around in a circle? Do you go forward in a straight line? Or do you take that line and cause it to spiral upward, ever upward, in a spiralling escalation to the Light Absolute?

Where do you go? You go to the Sun Absolute. How can you go to the Sun Absolute when you have lingered in the shadow? The shadow is any moment of inconsistency in your life that comes from allowing your world condition to impose and impinge itself upon you. The world can be anything, from a motorized vehicle to a business associate to a stranger in the street who cries out in his attempts to take you into his struggle. Do not be taken in. Give Light to the degree that he is able to accept the Light and move quicky onward.

Power factors (individuals with developed Light Absolute), are rapidly being built now by the Great Architect in order that the structure of the great building of consciousness for the light of the new age may be completed. Conceive, if you will, that the Grand Architect is constructing this building of stupendous magnitude with the use of pinpoints, diamond points, star-points of light, connecting beams of light, structuring the foundation deep within the Earth, and building it stage upon stage into infinity.

The Grand Architect looks to the right and to the left, above, below, all around, for those who are actively taking a role in building their own Light Absolute. And he thus moves each of those star-points of light into place.

Then the great structure begins to move. For it is not a static structure. It is dynamic — moving, moving great vortexes of energy above, upward, into the Sun Absolute.

The Grand Architect does not have to do his work alone. The Lords of the Sun Absolute, who long since have built their Light Absolute and reached high rank in the hierarchy, look upon this structure that is being built, find it good, and begin to participate. These lords give to the structure —

which is being built upward from the earth — a new dimension of the Light Absolute. Now it is being formed from above and below.

This planet upon which you dwell has the possibility of becoming one of the great planets of your solar system. In truth, when this structure which the Grand Architect is now building is complete, it will create a glistening Light Absolute emanating forth from the planet Earth, blending with the Sun Absolute, creating paradise itself on Earth. Thus, Earth will become one of the great jewels of the kingdom of the heavens.

You may think that you are only a speck, less than a speck, of dust in the universe. That speck of dust, when it is brightened into a pinpoint of light, a diamond of light, a star-point of light, is essential to the plan of the Grand Architect.

Think not lightly of your role, my friend. Think of your role as being significant to the degree that were you not to become, to *be,* the Light Absolute, then the very foundation of the structure would be shaken. For how can the Architect build the building unless all of the building materials are perfect? *Be ye therefore perfect, even as your Father in heaven is perfect.*

In the process of perfecting your presence, your pinpoint, your diamond-point, your star-point of light, forget not to be in delight, in joy, in happiness. For the Grand Architect would never want you to take life so seriously that you forget to be joyful. Then you would not be a bright light; you would be strong, perhaps, you would be powerful, perhaps, but where would be the light? Be delighted with life, be joyful, do delightful things. Be happy, laugh, smile. Be in the gloriousness of life. The gloriousness of life is joyful.

The teachers and the angelic ones dwell not in sadness, not in austerity, but in such pure delight that moment-by-moment the ever-present radiance of God beams forth. As you are in the power of the Light Absolute, you connect with those who are also in that power. (See Chapter 16, "Ultimate Individuality.") And the joy is fulfilled.

Chapter Four
Spiritual Energy

We will consider the world as an energy system. Every animate and inanimate object contained within or on the surface of Earth is an energy system, and all of these energy systems interrelate so as to give the appearance of one solid whole.

Man, in the unfoldment of his evolutionary process on Earth, is an energy system. He is made up of a complex set of energy values. First, there is his physical energy system, which is experienced through the blood circulation, the breath, the digestive process, and mental energy structure. Moreover, man has access to an energy that he rarely, if ever, utilizes — spiritual energy.

Spiritual energy is made up of the substance of God, reduced to proportions suitable for man to utilize without overcharging. The spiritual energy is available at all times in all places, no matter where man is on the face of the Earth or in the heavens. There is no place where spiritual energy is not. To reach into and utilize this spiritual energy should be every aspirant's challenge. Man should not struggle with fatigue, sickness, mental depression, or astral illusion. The only reason for this struggle is that he forgets the great vat of spiritual energy available to him, the great vortex of power ever his to call upon.

Let us examine the processes whereby man may tap this spiritual energy. First, recognize that the energy is available at all times. Second, recognize that the energy never imposes itself upon you. It must always be requested. Third, develop methods whereby this spiritual energy may be commanded. Fourth, apply those methods so that at all times this resource of energy is utilized.

There are three particular methods for commanding spiritual energy. The first is the unification of the physical-astral-mental energy bodies into one synchronized whole. This comes about by deliberate rhythmic breath control, not only when you sit quietly to contemplate or meditate, but throughout the day. You teach your breathing vehicle to partake of pranic life force energy through deep rhythmic breathing at all times.

Obviously this requires much attention, for the body breathing apparatus is accustomed to being lazy. In the beginning stages, the student will perhaps not be able to practice this rhythmic breathing faculty more than a few minutes per hour. If he will take those few minutes and, no matter what he is doing, inculcate within his awareness, *"Breath, I breathe,"* and do a number of short quick breaths, then one long deep breath, he will begin to teach the breathing faculty to do its job in a better way. So the breath would go: short breath, short breath, short breath, short breath — up to twelve short breaths — then one long breath.

This technique will cause the breathing apparatus to change its lazy cycle. It is the beginning of realizing the value of taking more pranic energy through the power of breath. It creates a new device for utilizing the higher spiritual energy.

The second method requires dedicated concentration upon the movement of the body in some rhythmic exercise, such as Tai Chi Chuan or some other yoga practices, followed by ten to fifteen minutes of pranayama breathing (alternate nostril breathing). Follow this with the seven-cycle breath, which is one deep inhalation, holding to the count of seven, and one exhalation holding to the count of seven, repeating the cycle seven times. This is one of the most unique breaths for breaking through the crystalized, hardened patterns that exist in most individuals and eliminating laziness of the breathing habits.

The third type of breath to be utilized is the breath of exertion, a deep panting breath, moving the diaphragm quickly in and out until finally the exertion is so great that it comes to a stop voluntarily. Following this breath you sit in deep meditation. This, done as a consistent daily program, will move the individual into the new form of spiritual energy.

Now we hasten to add that these exercises will be totally useless unless they are done diligently, day by day by day. It is far better not to start them at all than to do them spasmodically and irreverently. Moving into the spiritual energy is a very reverent activity. You are making contact with your own

Christ Being; you are making contact with your God Self. You are fusing your God Self and your ordinary human self. You are lifting your ordinary human self to the higher regions of experience.

You are, in other words, preparing for the complete transformation of your lower vehicles into the higher vehicle of light substance. Once you have practiced the moving of ordinary energy into spiritual energy, you will be given, from your own inner being, higher and more advanced instruction. You cannot be given this instruction from your own inner being until you have made the preparation to achieve it.

Moving into the spiritual energy system enables the student to bypass astral energy, which is detrimental energy. Most individuals, even those who are seekers of the way, are so immersed in astral illusionary energy, which is permeating the atmosphere at this time because of humanity's great psychosis, that they cannot function even at twenty percent capacity. One role of the fourth dimensional teachers is to stir as many aspirants as possible to defuse and remove astral illusionary energy from their systems, and guide them into the utilization of the higher spiritual energy.

The rewards are obvious. To be reborn, to be transformed, to be uplifted, to be *conscious,* to be God-centered, to be Christ-aware, to be inspired, to *be.*

Part Two
Communication With
Other Dimensions

Chapter Five
Interdimensional Communication

Let us consider specific ways of interdimensional communication:

Think of Who you are. You are an individualized aspect of God — Infinite, Cosmic, Creative Intelligence. Your individuality has been highly refined since its inception eons ago. There are no two of you alike. Perhaps we might say your individuality is the most precious, the most divine, gift of life. From the original flame, that source that gave you cosmic birth, you have traversed many planes of awareness and comprehension to arrive at the point where you can be of your refinement as an individualized aspect of God.

When you breathe, the breath you breathe is *your* breath. No other entity can breathe that breath for you. When you walk, the footsteps are your footsteps. No other individual can walk the mile for you. When you make what you consider errors or mistakes, they are your mistakes and must be corrected by you. While you are free to receive guidance from others on how to correct those mistakes, no one can make the corrections but you yourself. When you procreate, you unite for a brief moment in time with another individualized soul, and there comes forth from you a new creation, which must, by its very nature, individualize and become one alive.

The nature of the divinity expressed within you is such that wherever you go on your planet you must have a name.

Naming is so universally accepted that even when individuals leave this planet, or any other planet of a similar genre, they carry into higher regions a name that becomes blended with what might be called the soul name. Your individuality is such a precious gift that prayers of thanksgiving should be offered for it.

As individuals evolve into higher dimensions of awareness while occupying a physical body, they develop within themselves a faculty, dormant though it may be, for communicating with spheres beyond the third dimension. This development is a part of the individualization process. Yet most people go from birth to so-called death without ever activating this faculty.

The capacity to communicate with dimensions beyond the ordinary human dimension enables you to develop deeper and more profound understanding of the very nature of the cosmos. While you are housed in a third dimensional body, you are limited by the comprehension of your mind as it has been structured from birth, and by the comprehension of the society in which you move about. To remove that limitation you may, if you choose, develop the capacity for higher dimensional communication.

Now to speak in specifics. You have in your communication system the understanding of yourself as an individualized soul and as a complex of bodies. The first specific step to take in order to prepare yourself for the possibility of interdimensional communication is to *integrate and synthesize these bodies.* You know of your physical body. You have heard of your etheric body, mental body, astral or emotional body, causal body, and so forth. As discussed in the chapter on spiritual energy, it is unlikely that you could have consistent communication with the higher realms if, for instance, you dwell mostly in your physical body or mostly in your mental body or mostly in your emotional, astral body. It is only when these bodies are first understood and then integrated that you begin to develop the powerline through which you can communicate with higher dimensions. This is done by meditation, and by spiritual alignment, as already discussed. (See Chapter 4, "Spiritual Energy.")

The specific step for the development of this faculty is commitment with regularity to *the practice of the presence of God in your life.* We can break this down into two general aspects.

First, continuously, or as often as possible, remind yourself, in all circumstances, "God is now expressing through me at this moment." The second aspect of practicing the presence of God is to set aside and dedicate certain portions of time with regularity to indwelling and to realizing the faculty as it is opening. In other words, certain times of contemplation and meditation.

A third specific is *the study of the nature of subtler energies,* for how can you relate to these subtle energies unless you understand their basic nature? So you begin to seek out literature that speaks to you of the various dimensions. If you can find literature that you can completely respect and with which you feel at home, it will be of untold benefit in understanding the subtler dimensions.

The fourth specific is this: for a relatively long period of time, which only you can determine, you decide to *set aside all prejudices, all doubts, and all logical explanations.* As long as you feel that there must be a logical explanation, you will not be able to experience fully the nature of interdimensional communication. While there is great value to logic and to the use of the reasoning mind, for the exploration of the awakening super-faculty employed in interdimensional communication (a faculty that you might call intuition, although it goes beyond intuition in the usual sense) there must be freedom from logical analysis.

The fifth specific, we will call, for want of a better term, *resting in the awareness that the faculty is even now functional.* "Resting in the awareness" means that you do not struggle, you do not argue with yourself, you do not chastise yourself because evolution is not happening faster. You rest in the awareness that this divine apparatus was long ago bestowed upon you but has been dormant and that you are now in the process of allowing it to awaken.

Now to consider the value of interdimensional communication. Perhaps you have noticed that prevailing world conditions about you are, to put it mildly, volatile. Highly disruptive would be a better description. Such world conditions will continue and increase as the year 2000 approaches, although these conditions actually have to do with cosmic time calendars, not man's. As you approach the turn of the century, which is a hair's breadth away, you will increasingly need higher dimensional information. If you try to cope with the cataclysmic events about to occur in your world, in fact, even now occurring, with ordinary knowledge you will be like sheep among wolves.

You must reach higher for the way through. There are all too few people prepared to counsel the hordes who will need guidance and survival techniques. If you find yourself in a crisis and seek help, depending solely upon ordinary human knowledge, that help will be very hard to come by. But if you know the art, the skill, the value of interdimensional communication, you can, in the midst of the worst catastrophe, whether it be psychological or physical, stand still, elevate your awareness, make contact with the higher dimensions, and obtain an answer.

It is the purpose of spiritual teachers to prepare as many people as possible, as quickly as possible, to have the awareness and the capacity for interdimensional communication. Impulses that you might think of as being like telegraph waves or radio waves are sent into a channel's mental apparatus and must be translated into vocal or written communication. Many people have the potential for this type of interdimensional communication;

however, the teachers are looking for more than the mere capability. They look for those who are ready to receive and use interdimensional communication impulses to make their own lives full and powerful. *Full* and *Powerful*. For powerful individuals are now, more than ever in the history of the planet, needed as stabilizing influences.

Think for a moment of being a powerful light. Think of that light being distributed in your particular field of influence. Then think of that light multiplying and being distributed further than that. For the people you influence silently become carriers of the light, and if you have even *one moment* in contact with an individual who is even partially receptive, and you speak silently the word "peace" or "love," that receptor will take that word into his own apparatus, even though it may not be greatly developed, and he will carry it to the next individual. Perhaps to many. So you see the value of taking each of these specific steps, incorporating them into your life, and working with them on a daily basis until you have become sufficiently imbued with the power of interdimensional communication that you will be one of a small army of communicators.

The way is clear; while you see on the one hand great devastation, you see, on the other hand, personages in high places making valiant, courageous attempts at peace on Earth. You see arms being put down; you see children being lifted up. The balance between light and dark is very critical at this time. But the Light is beginning to be felt.

There are elders among you. Some walk in physical bodies, some come and go in and out of physical bodies that they create for the purpose at hand. Some are totally invisible, and yet they influence you, if you will allow the influence, as much as if they sat beside you or stood beside you in the physical body. As you learn higher dimensional communication, you become more receptive to their guiding influence. The elder ones of whom I speak will never tell you how to solve a personal problem. They will never tell you where to go or what to do to escape misfortune. They will rarely tell you how to live, unless you have made a total commitment to them as disciples.

The elders give you *clarity of perception* that you may see for yourself how to make a decision, how to solve your personal problems, how to act in the midst of a catastrophe, or when to leave before a catastrophe occurs. They will give you the power of energy to keep yourselves in the highest state of perfected health, if you will receive it. They will imbue you with the capacity to engulf yourself in the sacred flame of divine protection so that no harm can come to you wherever you are. All of these capacities they will give to you, if you are a true receiver, if you have dedicated yourself to becoming clear, if you have specifically decreed yourself to be one of the servers in the plan of light.

Before departing from this subject, one final comment. Because you are reading these words, you are ready for this development. Among you are those who have already opened the faculty. Did not the Master say, "Seek and ye shall find. Ask and it shall be given unto you. Knock and the door shall be opened"? The way is clear; the information is available. Do with it as you will.

Chapter Six
Receptivity to Higher Dimensions

It is already a well-known fact that the unfoldment of a particular life requires that the individual be receptive to a constant stream of impressions from the environment. So we need not dwell on that. What we wish to examine is your receptivity to impressions coming from your own soul and to impressions from those finer vibrations surrounding you and containing the potential for changing the structure of the external mind, which you use in daily life.

It is now imperative that you begin to realize the nature of the impressions coming from the realm of the soul and the nature of the impressions you receive from those interested individuals who dwell round and about you in finer dimensions — your teachers, your guides, their mentors, and the angelic hosts.

For it is a fact that when you enter a process for uplifting yourself out of the realm of ordinary man, you activate the connection between your human self, your soul self, and those angelic ones who from the beginning took upon themselves, by mutual agreement, the responsibility for guidance and development of your externalized form. The word "form" means those physical, emotional, and mental aspects of your being used in your daily world, not your inner self.

A particular system is tried with each individual to achieve the finest possible contact for the reception of ideas with which the individual can work. Thus the individual can be lifted into the realm of the soul.

Consider the inner mind. When you close your physical eyes you go within. There you find a world unlike the world you live in. Having entered the inner world, you then prepare the vessel — the higher mind — for the food of spiritual knowledge. This vessel will be your receptacle for impressions from the inner world. It is the plate; it is the grail; it is the cup. And in that cup your teachers, those interested parties of highest dimensions, place the food for your spiritual ingestion.

Now that you have come forth as a clear and shining vessel, bring to your altar the following:

- a candle
- a crystal bowl to hold water, symbolic of pure spirit
- a clear bell, chime or gong
- a crystal prism, two or three inches in diameter, or a rough-cut crystal
- paper and pen

As you approach your altar, meditate upon the Christ light. See the reflection of the light in the prism as you hold it to the candle. Imagine that light as being symbolic of your own Christ consciousness. Conceive of your own inner Divine Light, and meditate upon this. Remember, you are preparing yourself as the vessel to receive inspiration from higher realms.

Specifically, the way of preparing the vessel is this: First, cleanse yourself of all impurities before you enter your chamber of meditation. Bask in the radiance of the sun and ask of the sun that all impurities be removed from your mind, body, and emotions. Ask from your own Divine Light, while you are in the presence of the sun, that this cleansing take place.

If the sun, which is your heavenly body, is not shining, then create the inner Sun, and dwell with that Sun, and ask that Sun to remove all impurities, that you may have a clear vessel to place upon the feast board, that the teachers may fill the vessel with the finest food. Then ring the bell three times. This is the first step.

Second, look into the crystal prism and then look into your mind and ask of that mind, "Are there any impurities left within, any impure attitudes, any distasteful thoughts?" Are you clear and clean to receive the food that God and Infinite Wisdom is even now preparing for you? You ask that the prism purge you of any such thoughts, and the prism, having taken on a life of its own, then does its task and purges you of those residual thoughts. If you find any residue left, you do another cleansing, only this time it is an internal cleansing. You remain in the crystal consciousness that is inculcated into your being through contemplation of the crystal prism.

When you are finally cleansed you will know by the flow of clear thought of an inspired nature, which you then write upon your paper with free-flowing ink. When that inspired thought has come through, you are ready to enter your meditation chamber. Bring the thought forth and place it upon the altar as an offering to your teachers, your angelic ones, and as a gift to God. This new form of approaching your meditation chamber will make it possible for your teachers to fill your vessel with far richer food, of a finer substance, than that to which you are accustomed.

We call you now, oh friends of light, to prepare yourselves for the coming days of great transition from old ways to new ways, when your light becomes so bright, and your power becomes so stabilized, that your attendance will be to those greater powers as your teachers. And in a way that cannot be defined now, your attendance is essential to the completion of their work, that work done for the greater good of humanity.

You are asked to understand that your mind is naturally telepathic, impressionable and receptive when uninhibited by crystallized thought forms and prejudices. It is your responsibility as students of the "Way of the Light" to decrystallize your fixed attitudes and realize your ultimate receptivity to higher realms.

The best possible text on receptivity, which fortunately makes it unnecessary to expound upon the subject further, is a little but powerful treatise titled *Telepathy and the Etheric Vehicle,** which was dictated by the Master Djwhal Khul. I recommend that you obtain a copy of this treatise and study it thoroughly.

Impressionability is a gift if it is used correctly. Protect your vessel, cherish your vessel. When you do not stand before the beings of light, surround yourself with an impenetrable light, secure in knowing that you will be ready for your next communion.

And so you serve, to the purpose of being receptive to higher dimensional awareness. And so the consciousness of the Christ is developed. For the consciousness of the Christ is loving service. Through receptivity, as disciples you truly align with the spiritual hierarchy of the planet. And thus you serve.

---

*By Alice A. Bailey, Lucis Publishing Company, New York.

Chapter Seven
Immortality

Interdimensional communication places man in the realms of finer reality. Here his true potential begins to open to him. He catches a glimpse of his true nature. And thus it is time for us to discuss man's potential for immortality, the origin of the human idea of mortality, and the plan of the future.

The gods, the lords, the avatars, were *born* aware of their immortality and are not subject to confusion about it, because they do not have animal bodies. Man evolved long after the birth of the gods, out of the heart of the one great God. Man had from his inception the concept of mortality because of his physical heritage and his observation of nature. This situation is not without purpose, since it eventually leads to mastery of the physical element.

If you consider man as only a physical being, having come from the dust, molded out of the Earth itself through eons of evolution, from the mineral kingdom into the plant kingdom, then into the animal kingdom, and finally into man, you will note that through all of these kingdoms there is the perpetuation of life through the dual processes of life and so-called death.

The rock is born out of the bowels of the Earth, and after eons of evolution it becomes dead to its former self, transported into the ocean as grains of sand. The tree takes nourishment out of the mineral kingdom, and after a hundred or more years it dies and returns into the Earth as minerals itself. The animal has nurtured itself — whether it be the elephant, the dog, or one of the other animal forms — from the plant kingdom. With the exception of those that eventually become carnivorous, the animal evolves by the use of the plant kingdom. Certain forms of animals and certain forms of mammals from the sea evolved through the eons to form early man, and thus human evolution was accompanied by consciousness developing through the process called death and life. And so from the inception of the human kingdom, death has been imbedded in the idea of the evolutionary process.

Humans cannot conceive of themselves as being exempt from death. They therefore conceive of themselves, if they wish to cling to the idea that they are worthwhile in the evolutionary process, as achieving immortality of the soul.

Humans think nothing of the death of a tree. In fact, they consider it to be appropriate for trees to die to provide them with shelter. They think nothing of the death of an animal; they think it appropriate for the animal to die to provide them with food. Humans think nothing of the death of any of the plants that exist upon the Earth, for they think it appropriate for those plants to first take nutrients out of the mineral kingdom, to store them, and to make them accessible to humans as food.

So to humans the whole process of birth and death is as natural as the process of breathing while in the mortal body. The structuring of this human-racial-consciousness is so deeply imbedded that it seems to mortals truly impossible to change it.

And so, from many immortal states of life, from various realms of the universe, gods came to assist in the evolution of man — gods to populate the Earth, to teach man, and to raise his consciousness so that he could realize his potential for being as the gods. They came at the request of the Godhead, the One Supreme Being, Creator of All. The plan was that after the gods had helped man realize his potential for divinity, they would leave to let him develop without interference.

In the process of helping man, many of the gods went so deep into matter that they forgot their immortality and did not leave. And so they too had to begin the same process that they had taught the humans, which was to learn to be immortal. This forgetting of immortality by some of the gods — although not by all of the gods — created a dilemma indeed.

The gods who had remembered their immortality felt great concern for the gods who had forgotten. Gathering together all of their resources they tried in all sorts of ways not only to remind their contemporaries of their immortality but to encourage them to return to their immortal state of being in their finer bodies. For thousands of years the gods who had remembered worked with all diligence to remind the gods who had forgotten. Finally they saw that it was not possible, and they returned with great sadness to their own immortal kingdoms. They were told by the One Supreme Creator that all was not lost but that as those immortals who were left upon Earth cohabited with humans, they would take on attributes of the human, and the humans would take on attributes of the gods. And so there would be a blending. And after both humans and the gods who were left had made the descent so totally into the density of matter that there was no further to go, they would begin the ascent upward. And the gods would bring with them those humans who had the potential to realize their divinity and the nature of immortality.

Thus you have upon this planet in this era gods who have forgotten their immortality, or only have faint glimpses of it, and humans who are trying to realize their immortality and discard the ancient concept of death. Cooperating in the effort to help, from what you might call a distance, are the gods, the lords, the masters, the avatars, who dedicatedly assist the One Supreme Creator in penetrating into the consciousness of humankind the nature of its divinity. This effort of restoring the gods to their immortality and inculcating the minds of humans with their divinity and their potential for immortality will never be abandoned. The cause will never be deserted, for the request of the Supreme Godhead is that salvation, as it is called, will always be at hand for every human as a part of the work of the gods, the lords, the avatars.

At one point it was decided in conclave that the door to the human kingdom must be closed until a future time. Therefore, animals can no longer enter the human kingdom. They must wait until the humans who are already going through the incarnation process have either been dispersed into other areas to learn more of the nature of their own potential, or until the humans have indeed entered through the door of recognition — through the door of salvation.

Thus you see upon Earth today certain animal species attempting to become extinct, because their group spirit and their group avatars know that there is no hope for them to enter the human kingdom soon, and they are unwilling to wait. Therefore, they are trying to take their wave of consciousness into another planetary embodiment. The ones who have attempted to become extinct, such as your great bengal tiger and the great herds of buffalo that once roamed your continent, have been thwarted by man.

You can well see that if inhabitants of the animal kingdom were allowed to enter the human kingdom before those of the human kingdom had realized their divinity and moved on into higher states of being, there would indeed be great congestion in the human kingdom. And there is already great congestion and great travail.

What do you see happening? It is most interesting that more and more domestic animals are being developed. One day in the distant future the door into the human kingdom will once more be opened. And so some group spirits chose to enter into the environment of the human kingdom as domesticated pets. There they do their best to assimilate the qualities of humans, making preparation for that day, perhaps eons from now, when they may enter. Many of those animals, when they finally enter the human kingdom, will have advanced intelligence, because of their willingness to serve the human kingdom while they wait their turn to enter.

From the perspective of the higher realms it is a most interesting situation. Thus for man to strive for immortality is for him to realize his potential godhood, and for those immortals, those gods and goddesses with whom you walk unknowing, to remember their divinity and return to their immortal state of being is a major undertaking. The humans who instinctively know them to be gods will cling to them with all their might, and naturally so, for when that one you know as the Christ walked among you, did not the multitudes cling to Him for the very light of His presence?

There are needed upon Earth at least two hundred or more realized immortals, for without the realization of immortality the immortal is simply a human. With two hundred or more realized immortals, the power balance can change. Wars can cease. Crime can be abolished. Retardation and all forms of deformity can vanish from the Earth. Discontent, greed, avarice, maliciousness, envy — all of the deadly sins — can cease to exist if enough of the gods, the immortals, realize their immortality.

And if humans who have the greater vision can achieve their immortality while occupying their physical bodies, a paradise can then exist upon Earth.

Chapter Eight
The Nature of Shambala

In the vast plains of the Gobi desert, in the realm of the etheric, is the place in consciousness known as Shambala. Shambala is a great arcane city of luminous texture in which reside in fourth dimensional awareness many masters, teachers, angelic ones, workers, and divine beings.

Shambala is the residence of the Lord of the World, Sanat Kumara (not to say that the great lord is embodied in the physical, for he is embodied only in the etheric). The great Lord Sanat Kumara, dwelling in his etheric body above the Gobi desert, in the arcane city, has multiple manifestations of his etheric body energy. He has the capacity for the reproduction of the energy to a very fine form or the expansion of the energy to a very amazing, magnificent form.

The city contains great halls of learning, beautiful centers of art, powerful stations of scientific enterprise, great generating power centers for the maintenance of balance throughout the planet on the etheric level. From Shambala emanate all of the seven rays on which humanity is destined to evolve. The Lords of the Rays are in conclave with regularity with the Lord Sanat Kumara. Magnificent halls of learning embody the findings of the Lords of the Rays as they work with the evolutionary process of humanity.

Any individual who aspires to the light may enter the realm of Shambala at will, but he will not be allowed to go into the deeper chambers. He will only be allowed to walk the paths of golden light and to go into certain chambers, according to his degree of understanding and awareness. Teachers who reside in the Shambala energy invite their students periodically to take part in the great festivals that emanate from Shambala throughout the planet. The rays go not only across the planet on the physical level but interpenetrate the depth of the planet on the etheric level. In other words, those ray energies go through the Earth. There is, in fact, emanating from Shambala the energy equivalent of the whole physical world — in etheric form.

Shambala is operating through solar and cosmic energy, which is taken into great generators on the cosmic level, multiplied, and disseminated to man on the physical level. Unfortunately man has misused much of this energy.

The purpose of Shambala is threefold. First, to maintain the power for the functioning of the planet. Second, to emanate ray energies that will inspire the minds of man. And third, to be a unifying force between man and the Creator.

If you were to go for a walk in Shambala on the

etheric level, you would see, very much to your surprise, many buildings quite similar to those in your larger cities, except that they are built with etheric substance. There are towering multi-storied buildings, which must be reached by a sort of etheric elevator. There are streams of energy conveyors, like conveyor belts, which move the people to and from and around the city. The bodies of the people who reside there for the most part are very similar in form to the bodies of the people who reside in physical bodies on Earth, except that they do not need the same digestive or intestinal apparatus necessary for the dense physical body.

Great harmonic sound emanates at all times from Shambala, and the ear that is attuned to the Shambala energy is blessed indeed. Thought-provoking activities take place in the great Shambala center, and many scientists and statesmen of the planet Earth not presently in physical embodiment dwell there and frequently meet in conclave to resolve or attempt to resolve many world problems.

A portion, but not all, of the great hall of Acca, where the records of all humanity are kept, will be found in Shambala. Picture a great cosmic library with rows and rows of halls of records, aisles full of records, cabinets full of books, where great scrolls containing the history of man can be laid out on tables to be read. Scribes and recordkeepers dwell there, as do representatives of all forms of science, of the healing arts, of education, of diplomacy and statesmanship, and of ceremony and magic.

Power centers are constantly being built and

rejuvenated in Shambala in order that their functioning energy may assist in the evolution of the inhabitants of Earth. Were the great golden light of Shambala to be extinguished even for one minute, Earth itself would collapse and become a dead planet. The vortex of power that exists in Shambala is great indeed.

It behooves the individual who is walking upon the path of light, as well as individuals who aspire to walk upon the path of light, to daily attune to the great Shambala energy, to be aware of that great power structure over the Gobi desert, and to say, *"I ask that my Divine being be fed and blessed by the power of Shambala, that my human being, that body being in which I am presently encased, may become lifted up and that my mind may be enlightened by the energy of Shambala."* Such prayers are clearly registered in Shambala and are answered by the bringers of good from the Shambala station.

For it is like a great way station through which all types of traffic go. Human souls come and go through Shambala on their way to and from embodiment upon Earth. Shambala is the place from which many monumental discoveries are made and brought to Earth, or sent to Earth, according to the situation. Sometimes personages of fame from physical incarnation, who need to enter a rejuvenation center, will go directly to Shambala upon the death of their physical body and will dwell there for a hundred years or more, assimilating the Shambala energies and preparing to make new embodiments from those Shambala energies.

Shambala was created many hundreds of thousands of years ago, but it is not as old as the Earth itself. It was created specifically for the purpose of housing intelligent activities having to do with the evolution of the elder brotherhood. These elder ones, sitting in the stately presence of each other, send out their form, energy, light, love, peace, order and harmony to all humanity. Some humans receive it, some let it go by the wayside.

There are other power centers on the planet in the etheric realm, but Shambala is the greatest, and it nurtures all of the others. In almost every mountain range of any major consequence, you will find a center of power in the etheric realm, and each one of these centers of power receives its originating power from the great Shambala valley.

Many people travel across the Gobi desert without even being aware that the arcane city of Shambala exists. This is as it should be. Perhaps one day the area will be surrounded by a luscious valley and the Gobi itself may be converted from desert to fine grassland and then finally to beautiful farmland. But for the time it is seen as a desolate place, and only a few know of its grand nature on the etheric level.

Life is a mystery, one to be solved by he who seeks. Seek the mystery of Shambala, and you will obtain much understanding of life. Evoke and invoke the mystery of Shambala, and you will lift yourself up out of desolation into light.

Part Three
Making It Work
For Individual
Evolution

Chapter Nine
Land·Water·Air

Picture the point at which water, air, and land meet. Hold this image clearly in your mind for a moment. Ocean meets land; air meets ocean; land meets air. Stand upon the shore where the ocean meets the land and mentally inculcate the feeling of immersion in the air at this point where land and water and air meet. Feel the air substance around you. Sense the water of the ocean gently lapping upon your feet. Feel the pull of gravity as the land holds you fast.

Bring your attention to an absolutely focused point where the three meet. Land — water — air. This is not such a difficult exercise. It is one that you can experience in a moment of thought. Land, water, air. Land, water, air. Point of focus: land, water, air.

The great malady of man is that he has lost the capacity to have such a distinguished, distinctive focusing of thought. Your instructions have placed your attention upon the meaning of power. You have given your attention fully and completely to the meaning of the Sun Absolute, and you have, just now, given your attention to land, ocean, and air. Now it is proposed that you apply the same focused attention on any given subject or any given object, and through the power of focused attention bring it into being, as you desire it.

Focusing your attention upon any given object and drawing that object to you is as simple as focusing your attention on the junction point of land, water, and air. The power of the universe lies at your fingertips. The power of the Sun Absolute lies within your realm of experience.

Your immediate realm of experience is the world. The material substance where you find yourself housed functions in the material world that is all around. Yet your material substance also functions in etheric realms.

Material substance cannot exist unless first it has been conceived in etheric substance — in mind substance. When you put your attention upon the idea of land-water-air, you are not on the land at the ocean experiencing the air, yet the experience is as real as if you were there. You are focusing your attention in the etheric realm, the realm of mind, and you are creating a reality in the physical realm. Everything upon which you place your focused attention must happen upon the etheric level first.

You have learned that power starts with the *realization* of your own power. Having this realization, it is only necessary to make use of the tool of focused attention to demonstrate the power and achieve results.

If there is an object that your heart desires, focus attention upon land-water-air and then focus attention upon that object. You will have developed sufficient power of concentration from several minutes of focused attention upon land-water-air to transfer that concentration to the object of your desire and achieve results on the physical plane. Let us say that you have a malady that needs to be healed. Practice first the focusing of your attention for several minutes upon land-water-air, thus bringing the mind to an absolute point. Then turn that same focused attention toward the healing, and the healing will take place.

Let us try another experiment. Turn your attention to a desert island, far away, in the beautiful South Pacific. There are no dwellings or people in sight. There is only the water, the sky, the palm trees, the land, and your body, anchored by gravity, upon the shore. The sea is an exquisite blue; sky meets sea at the horizon. You are alone. You raise your arms to the heavens and allow the sun to beat upon your chest. You move your toes in the sand, reminding yourself that you are of Earth. Yet, as your arms are extended upward, you are of sky, and as you extend your arms outward you are of the sea.

Turn and walk upon the land. Select a sturdy tree and walk deliberately toward that tree. As you approach the tree, extend your arms outward to the tree. Walk directly to the tree until your body is aligned with the trunk of the tree. Now place your arms securely around the tree and pretend for a moment that you are that tree. Say, as you hold the tree, "I am this tree. I am this tree. I am this tree. This tree am I."

Feel the movement of the swaying fronds in the wind; *be* the tree. Forget all else. You *are* the tree upon the shore, upon the island. You are the tree. Sense what the tree experiences being rooted eternally to the ground, not being mobile, having only roots to hold it there. The only movement that the tree, which is you, can experience, is the movement of the leaves, of the trunk, and of the upper limbs in the wind. Sense the movement. Be that movement.

Now, release your attention from the tree, and realize that you are the man, you are the woman, that you were the tree only for a moment in your imagination. You have more than the tree has, for you have mobility. You can move your feet about. You can walk back to the shore; you can lie prone upon the sand and allow the sun to shine upon your body. You can rise, you can move toward the ocean, you can swim in its water. You can swim beneath the surface, as the fish do. You can hold your head above the water and swim back and forth. And finally, you can return on the crest of a wave to the shore. You can walk, you can run, you can move, you are a man, you are a woman!

All of that which you have just experienced took place through focusing attention in the etheric realms, the realm of higher mind, the realm of creative imagination. You tasted the salt air, you felt the water, you moved upon the shore, you became the tree, you returned to the shore, you realized, "Ah, how great it is to be a human being!"

Thus, through focusing your attention in the etheric realm you became one with a material substance, even though you were in ethereal substance. You will see, because of this momentary experience of total focused attention, that one day in the not-too-distant future you will indeed have the experience that you have just lived. Energy follows thought.

Teachers everywhere are attempting to guide man to this realization: That which you think propels, through focused attention, an impression on the etheric realm and is, through persistent focused attention, brought into material manifestation.

Power comes into your world, into your arena of experience, through the art and the skill of focusing attention. It is your responsibility on the path of being to realize the wholeness of your being through this focusing of the attention. Say to yourself, "I am the most fortunate of all creatures, for I have been gifted with a beautiful body vehicle, to experience in the realm of material substance that which is existent in the realm of ethereal substance. How grateful am I to have this privilege."

Cherish the power of the mind to focus attention upon land-water-air and then to move that attention to whatever is your object of desire. Though this may seem to be a simple lesson, rest assured that if you apply it in your daily life, you will create for yourself a paradise on Earth. By this means you are able to move from the third dimension into the fourth dimension, while still occupying the third dimension. This ability is multidimensional experiencing. All of those experiences that are of negative connotation, those evils that man would do unto man, those errors, those warlike actions, will cease to be a part of your realm. They will exist in a dimension that is unrelated to your new dimension.

Never again will you walk upon a shore without realizing the immensity and the simplicity of the thought that at that point where you walk, three elements come together in perfect synchronism: land-water-air. They form for you an environment of profound meaning. The fact that the ocean or the river or the stream can meet the land at a particular given point and be contained at that point and not go beyond that point is a miracle worthy of a lifetime of study. The very gravity that holds you to Earth — that also is worthy of a lifetime of study.

Initiates who step into the realm of light, who come from previous eons of evolutionary work, find themselves already equipped with all of these awarenesses. Old error patterns fall away totally, leaving the initiate in the way of light. Consider yourself fortunate to be an initiate upon the path of light.

Return often in your meditation to the concept of land-water-air. Hold in your mind the idea that all of your outer work is but a field in which you can express your inner nature. Growth comes through knowing and not through doing alone.

Chapter Ten
Discipline, Order, and Use of Time

The way of the world requires discipline. Discipline is not required by those in higher regions, as it has long since been learned and assimilated as a part of the being, just as breath is a part of the being when you are in incarnate form. It is the way of the world, however, that in order to accomplish any given task, the effort of discipline must be applied to that task.

The word itself is very interesting. If you think of the root of the word, you can easily see how it derives from the word "disciple". And when you think of a disciple, you can more easily grasp the nature of the word "discipline". A disciple is one who, having chosen the lighted way, orients himself in his daily living to do every action and to think every thought in terms of his discipleship. In the way of the world, this commitment requires much attention to any portion of life in which accomplishment is desired.

You cannot accomplish unless you apply yourself to the task at hand, whatever it might be. The word "discipline" also implies, according to worldly standards, *hard work*. Many times discipline is overlooked because the two are engrained in man's consciousness as synonymous.

Most people are looking for easy work rather than hard work, and so the word discipline in modern context has become disliked. It has become an abomination. In society today are multitudes of undisciplined people who can only be controlled by virtue of laws enforced upon them.

Much of humanity is now looking for that final disciplinarian who will say, "Do thus and so. Think not for yourself, my friend. I will do your thinking for you. All you need to do is follow what I have set up for you to do." Thus the masses of humanity have escaped self-responsibility and have become totally dependent upon the state as the authority to discipline them. It is easy for them to conform to discipline imposed from the outside; it is difficult for them to conform to self-regulated discipline.

It appears, from every vantage point of those who dwell in higher dimensions, that the world, regardless of the disarray evident on one level, is an orderly place. Even in the regulation of the masses of humanity, through laws imposed upon them, there is a certain orderliness. But that orderliness, unfortunately, comes across as control. And as that control is exerted over masses of humanity, they succumb more and more to this discipline imposed from outside.

Each of you who has come forth into the path of light and who has taken up one stage or another of discipleship, long before this incarnation, is now finding himself in a very unique position. You are finding yourself in the position of being able to say, "For this moment in time, I am I. And I may, at any given moment in time, bring forth from my inner nature that capacity, that great well of creativity, which will free me from the evolutionary wheel of the masses."

This, indeed, should be every aspirant's desire. It should be every disciple's main goal while in incarnate form to raise his consciousness from the level that locks him into mass evolution and to place himself upon the path of higher evolvement through self-discipline.

Looking at the universe we see certain basic fundamentals. First, God's universe is an orderly universe. The stars are in the heavens, the heavenly bodies rotate according to a definite plan, and there are elements in the running of the universe considered to be "scientific". There is a scientifically determinable basis for every movement, even for the growth of every hair upon the head of every individual.

Man is a cosmos. His body itself is a cosmos. His world is created according to the mental and emotional patterns that he sets up for himself. According to those patterns, he is either in control or out of control.

In order to achieve that next octave of your development as disciples, first it is essential that you begin the continuous study of the meaning of the two words "orderliness" and "discipline". Second, it is necessary for you to invoke patterns in your lives that are self-perpetuating by their very nature. Patterns as simple as these: early rising for greatest accomplishment and planned daytime activity for the sense of fulfillment at the end of any given day. How the day starts helps determine how it will go. Finally, at day's end review the day's activities to see whether that goal which you set for yourself upon arising has been accomplished.

These routines structure into your daily life, and thus into your whole life, a pattern. That pattern will lead you most clearly into a sense of accomplishment.

You are not in a religious monastery; you are in the monastery of the world. You are possibly in the most difficult situation, for you are bombarded on a daily basis with those mass hypnotic, powerful, vibratory emanations of humanity, congested into cities. Yet you have, from the level of your soul, placed yourself here so you may experience your own magnificent potential to emerge from the densest form of matter into your eternal light body being.

As you make this transformation, you assimilate into your soul qualities that will stay with you throughout your eternal evolution. As soon as you are able to live a true life, fully aware of your godliness within the midst of density, then you will be removed from that density — not by death, but by enlightenment.

To try to escape from that density in order to achieve a state of orderliness is foolhardy. The only place that discipline can be invoked is where you are. If you are in the darkest dungeon, you can invoke the discipline of using the mind for creative purposes. If you are on the top of a mountain, you must then invoke the discipline for acquiring adequate oxygen to maintain your physical body. If you are lost at sea on a raft with no compass, then you will need discipline to find your way to a shore through the study of the heavenly bodies at night and sun during the day.

There are many places in which invoking that discipline would be ten million times harder than where you are. Suppose that you had been placed in deepest Africa where all around you were natives who had no understanding of you or your language system. Then you would have to invoke discipline in order to find your way out or to find a way to live in harmony with the tribes. Suppose that you had been born into a race of pygmies, and you had the mind that you have now. Then you would have to find your way through that density, to evoke finally from within yourself release from that condition. Suppose that you had been born into the body of a mongoloid, with the mind that you have now. Then you would need that discipline to bring yourself forth, through whatever that mongoloid child must experience, to arrive at your body of light.

Many individuals have taken upon themselves such difficult situations and are even now working their way through such conditions. I give these to you as examples, to show you how fortunate you are that you designed the life that you have lived, and that you have come to the point where you are now, and that you may now be an example — yes, example. The word is chosen deliberately. For all who come near you may say, "Here is a stalwart person, for he or she lives in the world, yet he or she has the consciousness of a lord."

Perhaps the design given to you for your daily life should be expanded. Let us say you have before you a set of days, three hundred and sixty-five altogether. Set aside two days before the new year is officially ushered in and plan for the year in great detail, day by day, month by month, a calendar filled with all that you wish to accomplish. Fill it with your plans for the way that you are going to use each day, and you will be overwhelmed at the miraculous results at the end of the year. If you would do this you would be so inspired by what you saw laid out before you that you would be much more likely to accomplish your goals than if you only generalized about it, saying, "Oh, yes, in the next year I wish to complete this thing and that project."

It is the waste of daily activity that makes the waste of a month, and it is the waste of a month that makes the waste of a year.

Discipline and orderliness will accomplish that which you desire to accomplish before you are released from your physical vehicle, if you desire to be released in the future. You may find that if enough of you emerge to do what the elder ones have in mind, you will not want to leave your physical body because you will be living, in your dimension at least, in paradise on Earth. (See Chapter 7, "Immortality.") The world hysteria may go on, but you will have no part in it.

We said that the first fundamental principle is that God's universe is an orderly universe. If what the great Lord Hermes said, "As above, so below," is true, then it is inherent within each of you to have an orderly universe.

Orderliness means this: as you move about your space, whatever it may be, you see all around you the same motion that goes on in the cosmos. You see that each step that you walk is an orderly step, a disciplined step, toward the release of the soul itself from the confines of physical disaster areas. For when the body experiences disaster, the soul also experiences it. And the record must then be cleansed before the soul's growth can continue.

It is not that you must always have, as you say, every paper in its place. But you must use time as a great gift. You must use thought as a great gift. And you must not occupy your thought patterns with trivialities. You recognize the differences in people, and you make very sure that you do not mix your angelic forces with those whose evolving vibration is in disharmony to yours. You bless them by your presence, but you turn and go your way when they try to take you in, to be one with you because of your great light, which is emerging.

After orderliness, the second fundamental principle is that God's universe is a universe of light. As you work through discipline, you become a lighted being. For the teachers or spiritual guides, it is one of the most remarkable visions to behold you as you meditate, for you build these astonishing auric lights. The aurora borealis is nothing in comparison to you when you are centered in your fullness, in your God Self. It is a vision to the teachers, and one that they cherish. More of this, then, is needed.

In order that the "as above, so below" principle may work in your life, daily centering, not only once but more than once daily, is essential. Bodily perfection is essential. And you may find, as perhaps you already have found, that when you are in a major lifetime, with major disciplines you have invoked upon yourself, that your body will throw back certain conditions that are residues of conditions experienced in prior incarnations. And it is a part of your discipline that you must work through those, go beyond them, and be perfected in your body system.

You can work through the residual conditions in any way that you wish: through medical assistance, through prayer, through energizing, through spiritual healing, through chiropractic treatment — whatever way you may wish, but it is your infinite, unlimited responsibility to have your body as a perfect temple of the living God. It is essential that the body be your servant, and it is also necessary that you be its servant, that it may come into its fullness, through the power of your emotional and mental bodies being perfected.

We are talking about perfection, that great ideal that all men are born to strive for and that you accept moment by moment by moment as you evoke discipline into your life. Time, in the eternal sense, does not exist. Time, in the human sense, is of the essence. Once a soul decides to make the descent into matter and to take up bodily evolution, all discipline is needed to achieve that angelic state again. Throughout scriptures, no matter whether Buddhist, Hindu, Christian, Zoroastrian, or other, there is a common thread: "Discipline, discipline, discipline."

In order to remind yourself of the nature of discipline, take any scripture, go through it, and make notations of all of the various forms of discipline mentioned. From the various scriptures, a whole volume on the subject of discipline can be gleaned.

Discipline is not all work. Even to rest is a discipline. Yet even when difficult, discipline can be a joy. If you take upon yourself discipline as an angry "must", something that cannot be avoided, it will be to naught. It will be of absolutely no value. So discipline, then, must be joyful. It must be through laughter and delight that you see yourself moving in a disciplined and orderly way toward your goals.

Another facet of discipline involves contemplation. Each individual needs to develop contemplation as a part of his discipline. Contemplation may seem undisciplined; and yet, how can you contemplate any given thing unless you take yourself out of the scurry of daily living and place yourself in a situation where you can contemplate life and the nature of living?

Contemplation is musing upon any given subject. You take a subject — let us say truth, or light, or the cosmos — and you place yourself, through a meditative process, in a state of ease. It can be done while walking, while sitting, lying down, riding on a boat. You place yourself in an easy, thoughtful state, to contemplate the process of life around your subject.

Sometimes contemplation can be on life itself. Musing over the interesting aspects of life that move in your daily vision, wondering about the people around you, saying, "Who is this person? At what point is this person in his evolution upward? Was this person ever in the animal kingdom? What characteristics reveal this to me?"

Musing is often asking questions. Contemplation is sometimes asking questions. It is giving yourself over to a subject of your choice and dwelling with that subject until you begin to feel at home and at one with it. This is contemplation.

You can benefit much from contemplation if you allow yourself the time. To go forth to the great ocean and allow the sun glistening upon the ocean to absorb you, is that not contemplation?

Concentration, on the other hand, is much more focused energy. You concentrate when you focus on your paperwork. You concentrate when you study a book. You concentrate when you have a telephone conversation with someone, or at least it would be appropriate to concentrate to bring about the very best possible results of that telephone conversation. You concentrate when you write a letter because you want that letter to portray a certain set of facts or a certain feeling. So you concentrate so that the feeling may be expressed. You concentrate when you work upon any given task.

You can also perform acts of concentration in order to develop this ability more fully. One of the best acts of concentration is, when you awaken in the morning, to design your day before you arise. This is concentration upon your day. Another concentration is to review your day before you fall asleep. For how can you review the day without concentrating upon it?

You concentrate when you are lighting a fire. You have but one thought, the fire is to be lit. You may have some other fleeting thoughts, but basically you are concentrating when you light the fire or hold a lighted match to a candle. You are concentrating at that moment upon light.

Now, you may wish to make a comparison of the three — contemplation, concentration, and meditation.

How is meditation defined? There are many opinions on what meditation is. For our present discourse, let us say that meditation is dwelling with God, with no goals in mind, except immersion in the God Light through whatever means is appropriate to the individual. For once that immersion has taken place, then you are the flame, you are the fire, you are the torch, you are the Light, you are the Sun! What more is there to be?

We recommend that you explore the word, the subject of this discourse: *discipline.* Do not carry it as a burden upon your back and say, "Oh, if I do not discipline myself the teachers will vanish." What if the teachers vanish? Then *you* are your teacher. You are a great soul. You are perfectly capable of being your own teacher. In reality, this is your aim. You have all answers within you. Using wisdom you bring them forth into your daily life.

When you are in danger of being absorbed by the mass consciousness, which is lethargy, do not let it overcome you. Do not be taken in by it. That lethargy will overshadow you and overwhelm you and you will think it is your own. It is not your own. It is put upon you by the incomprehensible lethargy of mankind, a lethargy that goes against all of God's eternal planning. Yet, through free will, man has done it to himself.

Be not taken in. Rise, rise unto your own light. Exert that discipline over yourself that will take you into your own higher being. Then what will happen is that you will no longer need discipline, for you will be that which you have desired to be, and you will have absolved yourself totally from any of the mass consciousness surrounding and threatening to overshadow you.

Earlier we mentioned that many of you have placed yourselves in city environments that you may emerge out of them into the light. You are building within and around yourself a temple of power. Let that temple be so powerful that no force can come into it other than that which merges and blends with it. Then, when you move from where you are, you move that power with you. Oh, true, there is a residue left for the next individual who occupies the space where you were. But you take that power with you, and you begin to be a temple builder, on the etheric level, wherever you go. That temple is you. You are that temple. And you build it through the discipline of your mind, your emotions, and your body. You come into the realization of the fullness of the spectrum of your being.

Chapter Eleven
Work

Work is essential to the growth of man's inner being. Even the rich man, the man who has the fulfillment of all material needs, finds himself wondering what he can do to occupy his daily hours constructively. The value of work is immeasurable. The value of accomplishment is immeasurable. Accomplishment comes from the use of energy in effort put forth toward any given aim, project, or goal.

An individual has an idea. From whence the idea comes he knows not. The idea can be either stillborn, never to reach its culmination, or through a set of controlled circumstances, the idea can become a manifested reality. Always, between the thought or idea and the manifested reality, energy must be applied in what is commonly termed "work".

The word work can be applied to many things. To create a planet, for the angelic ones who have to do with the creation of planets, is work. To move the physical, mortal body from one point in space to another point in space could be considered work.

To place the mind's attention on the unfoldment of a given purpose and to follow that attentiveness with energy and effort could also be thought of as work.

Man's failing and shortcoming is considering work a negative thing and play a positive thing. It is work for a man to travel on the great river in a boat and to master the rapids. But because of the challenge of the adventure, he does not view this activity as work; he considers it play. His frame of reference determines whether a given task is work or play. Whenever man learns the art of placing his point of reference so that any task at hand becomes a source of enjoyment rather than a source of frustration and fatigue, he takes what is presumably work and changes it into play. Therein is the secret. When he sees the pure joyousness, when he realizes the oneness of himself with the purpose at hand, then the negative connotation of work ceases to exist.

The child is taught from a very early age, "You must work for everything you get out of life!" The very energy from which the instruction from the parent or the teacher comes carries negativity with it. So the child begins to equate work with the word "get" — two invisible negative elements that will control him all of his life. "You must work for what you get out of life." Immediately upon the permeation of this instruction into the child's mind, a resistance is set up to the idea of work and with it a fear that he will not get whatever it is that he wants. And so the process begins to be stressed over and over — the process of "working to get ". Thus the formative stages are tainted with this negative approach to acquisition of desired results through the exerted effort called "work".

A child is told, "You will find that the field of mathematics is one of the most exciting challenges to the mind ever presented to man. It is exciting to learn about the numbers and the system of numbers and see how they challenge the mind." Then the child expects delight, fulfillment, excitement, and challenge from mathematics. From that time on, if that instruction is continued, the child will mold his thinking to the exciting potential of mathematics. If, on the other hand, the child is told, "You must learn to add, subtract, multiply and divide, or you will be a failure in life," the child sets up the fearful expectation that he will not be able to learn basic arithmetic and that he will then be a failure in life.

As the individual becomes an adult, he carries with him an extensive amount of negative, adverse, ill-fitting instruction in his subconscious about various subjects. He is permeated with these stressful attitudes absorbed from parents, brothers and sisters, teachers, and society at large. Thus when he finally reaches adulthood, he no longer has an incentive for doing any activities that he associates with the stressful connotation of "work" — unless he is forced to do them by circumstances around him.

At some point every individual must identify this negative conditioning process, look at it carefully, and reverse its influence upon the life energy and upon the life form. If the individual does not do this, he sustains year after year the influence of those people who have long since gone out of his life but who have left their imprint upon it. Thus the expressions of highly intelligent adult individuals are often thwarted by people who are dead and gone.

Every individual who steps into the flow of divine awareness must eventually come at some point to a place where he willingly takes this past influence out, lays it upon the table, looks at it, and says, "I no longer need this attitude that came to me from some source that I know not, from some source that may be dead and gone. I no longer need this influence in my life. I will henceforth transform my attitude from one of despair to one of upliftment, and I will do this by turning work into play, sadness into joy, hatred into love, death into life."

Each moment that is spent in an attitude of despair about the work at hand is a moment of clutter and restriction. At any moment, man can look before him, see his tasks, duties, and chosen ideas for objective manifestation, and by applying the reverse procedure begin to think of these tasks as delightful fields of play. He can change the negative meaning of work into a feeling of delight, and he can move through any set of circumstances, no matter how difficult they may appear from the point of view of the world, in a sense of exhilaration, laughter, happiness, and sensitivity to his own inner being. This reversal is the challenge at hand for those upon the path of greater manifestation of divine awareness.

There is really no separation of the Self from the project, the idea, that is being manifested. Only the mind sees separation. Let the beauty of the Self experienced in the delight of play enter the beauty of the Self experienced in work, and you will see a complete change in the manifested form of what you are attempting to do. Time will pass quickly. The joy of the inner self will fill your outer being. And you will realize that you, in the process of accomplishing your given task, with song, with happiness, and with joy, have joined the angels as they accomplish their given tasks of creating planets, great and exquisite realms, for souls to experience. There is only a quantitative difference between creating a planet and creating a book. There is no difference between the Self of inner knowing and the self of outer doing. It is the level of consciousness that makes the difference.

In the preceding chapter, we discussed orderliness. This concept applies to work. Let us say that a scientist awakens in the morning at an early hour. Many things await his doing. His laboratory is before him. The first thing that the scientist must do is select the idea that he wishes to work on — whether it be for an hour or a day. He looks about him and sees that there is this idea or this formula. There is, perhaps, an idea for resolving a problem, an idea that is totally new and unexplored. If he looks upon the many ideas before him for exploration and unfoldment and becomes confused about what to do first, he will be confused throughout the rest of the day, and none of his experiments will be very effective. If he takes the first impulse and follows it, he will have a productive day.

He may not stay with the first idea throughout the day, but if he begins with the first impulse that he has, working with this formula or that formula, he will have a productive day, and his day will be filled with a flow of energy that cannot be stopped by outside interference. He will quickly attend to interruptions and then return to the project at hand.

Likewise, in the laboratory of life, each individual awakens in the morning with a certain built-up reserve of energy, which may be directed toward any set of ideas or just one idea. If he will follow the first impulse, quickly set himself to the task at hand, and then go from that to another, he will find that at the end of the day, in this laboratory of life, he has accomplished much in the way of effective work. He will find that his attitude toward what he has done will be sensible and sensitive. And he will find that at the end of the day he has more energy, if that is possible, than he had at the beginning of the day when he was first inspired. It is indeed the setting of the attitude at the entry into the laboratory that makes the difference.

Work is to be cherished. Work is to be consistently thought of as a privilege, a joy, and a gift of God. Let a person then review his attitudes toward work. Let him see that work can become play, that tediousness can be transmuted instantly into an attitude of excitement, and that accomplishment can come about more readily when the laboratory of life is thought of as a beautiful, glowing place, full of delightful adventure, rather than as a place of tedium and effort.

Chapter Twelve
The Inner Sanctuary

There is in every human being an inner monastery, a secret place that he can enter and separate himself from the world at large. Into this sanctuary he takes with him only the most cherished thoughts, the most pure ideals, and the most precious aspirations. For his own special moment in time he is a hermit, a recluse, a shramana. In his inner monastery he may meet with his God or with the emissaries of God who are aligned with him in higher dimensions. Thus he may conquer his lesser nature by the very act of subduing the senses and entering his holy place. The world of sensory experiences is reduced to a minimum and the world of light is enlarged. (See Chapter 3, "The Light Absolute.")

The sanctuary we speak of is a place within the inner being that we may enter through meditation or through any context of our life, but that we rarely do because of ignorance of its existence. The inner sanctuary has its outer manifestation in the monasteries that have existed throughout time, even in the days of ancient Egypt, as refuges to which individuals could remove themselves — to a sacred place that was prepared for them or that they prepared for themselves. In that environment, individuals could with their contemporaries seek to know the meaning of life.

As part of the evolution of man throughout time, monasteries have been built in secluded places, generally in mountains or at the seashore. Occasionally, a monastery exists within a city, hidden away, surrounded by city buildings. Whether secluded or part of the city, monasteries function as safe places in which to seek the inner light.

Modern day man needs to know more of his own inner sanctuary. Those who seek the path of truth, light, and oneness go forth *inward*. Going forth inward means to look at yourself from a place outside yourself, as you would look at your hand out in front of your face. And then carry that image of yourself to that still place within, your center.

When you start on the path, you recognize the debris with which you have surrounded yourself, the clatter and the clutter of modern day life, and you make a resolution: "I will put away for a certain period of time all outer confusion and I will enter into my own inner monastery, where I may dwell with the Light and with the beings of the Light who know of my existence but rarely have the opportunity to commune with me. As I enter the inner monastery, I will prepare myself by reading holy words, by dwelling with holy thoughts, and by realizing that central Sun within my own inner being, which is desirous of shining forth unto me."

Persons who have sought the inner sanctuary have various experiences to report. One has said that he has found the inner sanctuary in the very soles of his feet. Another has found it in the area of the solar plexus, while still another, in the middle of the brain. One man has found the inner sanctuary on the very tips of his fingers when he brought them together lightly, and a woman reported finding the special place outside herself, yet within herself, a serene lake without a ripple on it, with the sun shining brightly and no shadows.

Another has said that he experienced the inner sanctuary as a realization of a dot of light above his head. A woman found it as a brilliant sun approximately three feet in front of her third eye center. One man saw it as the light in the eyes of his dying father. As he recalled that light each time that he went into his inner sanctuary — the light of his father's eyes — it brightened before him and he knew that he had reached the place of his own central Sun.

There are an infinite number of ways that individuals can experience the inner sanctuary. For each it is to find his own way, his own spot of light, his own arc of Divine Light, or his own nonpresence of light. For sometimes in the great abyss, the absence of all things, the absence of thought, the absence of awareness of the body, the absence of any presence whatsoever, even the presence of light — there is found the inner sanctuary.

One most definite attribute of the inner sanctuary is that it is a wordless place. As long as words are chattering through the mind, the inner sanctuary has not been reached.

Various processes may be employed for going into the inner sanctuary. One is simply to absolve yourself through the flow of water upon your body, washing your hands of all external activities, symbolically cleansing the whole body. It matters not whether you lie down, stand, walk, or sit when you have prepared yourself to enter the sanctuary. It matters not whether you are in a house or in a church, or by the seashore, or at the top of a mountain peak. All that matters is that you know that you are leaving the world of outer reality and entering your own inner sanctuary.

The length of time that you stay within the inner sanctuary is entirely up to you. It is not a deciding process; it is a process of *experience*. As you experience the stillness, as you experience the sense of oneness with your own divinity, you may long to extend that experience for an hour or ten, for a day or a month. You may be unaware of the passage of time.

You will find that you have ebbs and flows in your capacity to remain within your inner sanctuary. Follow the ebb and flow. Because you go out and begin to have thoughts of various kinds does not mean that you cannot go back in again, for you can reenter the sanctuary by a simple exercise. Breathe deeply, hold for a moment, send that breath to the inner place, followed by thought, that then ceases to be thought but is "presence", the presence of knowing without expressing the knowing.

You can never invite another person into your inner sanctum, for your inner monastery is for you alone. It is invincible. It is that precious place in which you with God, as God, as God in you, as you in God, dwell. It is that place which no other living soul can enter. And when you are there you have the fullness of joy that is speechless, quiet beingness. To describe this joy in words is next to impossible. But to describe the invitation is imperative.

Once you have achieved and experienced the full realization of the power of your inner sanctuary remember the experience and savor it. Speak of it to no other human being. If you must share, share in a voiceless way to your own higher Self, to your God, to your higher being.

If others ask you, "What have you found that I have not found?" say simply, "I have found the inner sanctuary of my being." If they ask you to explain what you mean, say, "It cannot be described, it can only be sought, and the seeking is simple. The seeking is going forth within, and the going forth is looking at all external things around you and saying simply, 'These I can leave now to enter my inner sanctuary.'"

There is no other description that you can give to another person. For if you attempt to describe your inner sanctuary you will then be influencing their concept of their inner sanctuary. The best that you can do is to say simply, "May God be with you on your journey within."

Chapter Thirteen
A Safe Place in Spirit

We will consider now what we will call a safe place in spirit.

Man bungles about in his everyday world looking always for external events to solve his problems. He looks to this person and to that person, and he looks far and near to this situation or that situation, always externalizing his desire for a solution.

The truth is that solutions will never be found in the external world. Solutions must always be sought from within. A safe place in spirit develops as a direct result of the person recognizing the indisputable fact that there is no answer on the external plane. Having experienced the inner sanctuary (brief interludes of peacefulness), the realization comes that this state of being may be maintained almost constantly. This is the only safe place — a safe place in spirit.

When one decides to seek and dwell within the safe place in spirit, a kind of dying proceeds in the midst of continued bodily existence. Naturally the personal nature dreads this and grieves because it has to occur. The human personality longs to perpetuate itself in its conditioned state. But finally if the individual seeks without ceasing a safe place in spirit, a fire descends and consumes the personal ego. The fire does not destroy the personality — it transforms it. As a result of the flame comes a kind of dance of the inner being — a dance of joy, of light, of perpetual illumination. Then seeking solutions on the external plane obviously becomes of no importance.

When the seeker begins to live in the fire, in the flame of the internal safe place in spirit, at first the experience may seem excruciatingly painful. It continuously burns away all that the personality has clung to throughout life. Personal attachments seem to fall by the wayside. Then the individual finds himself saying, "Oh world, how sweet art thou that I must give thee up to the One Eternal Flame. The heat of the Great Sun even now burns away my attachment to thee. Oh world, in the current of bliss I release thee, yet ever I am with thee."

Through this transmuting process and this recognition of the safe place in spirit, an individual pierces into the higher level of consciousness. He becomes aware of his oneness with the infinite sea of consciousness and energy, which has been his from the inception of his being. From this inexhaustible supply, immediately and almost automatically, ideas and values pour forth into every area of concern in his life. So-called karmic obligations are infused with the power of the spirit, and the result is that the individual evolves toward his own higher being.

There is no doubt that such a safe place exists in the realm of spirit. But few are they who are willing to seek it out, and even fewer are willing to establish it as a sustaining point of being in their lives. No man enters the safe place in spirit without in some measure blessing the world through his achievement of finding that safe place. The really worthwhile life begins after the safe place in spirit has been established. The change is so great as to entirely reform the being within. The old self falls away. For the old self the great and baffling questions are gone. The soul's yearning is satisfied, and life's seeming tragedy is at last put to rest. So the awakening to the safe place in spirit is a death of the old and a birth of the new.

To find the safe place, the individual must first desire it. Superficially, an individual may seem even to himself to care most for external things, but very deep within he may have the inner desire. Ultimately, this deep inner desire for the safe place in spirit triumphs. Illumination breaks forth suddenly, spontaneously, without the personal consciousness being quite ready for it. The moment of transition from the old conditioned being to being in the safe place in spirit brings about a radical change in the visible outer life. Those things that mattered, that seemed of utmost consequence, no longer have any importance.

The inner being perfoms the action that is beyond the power of the unawakened spiritual person. It performs this powerful action because the individual requested it in one small moment within himself — when he realized that without achievement of the safe place in spirit all would be lost. And so within himself he reached out and asked that he might have a cosmic alignment. He thus invoked the active cooperation of his higher intelligence, and rather than the mere idle chatterings of the unawakened mind he begins to experience the glorious oneness of the merging of the human personality with the spirit. This development creates a vital power for awakening, for dwelling within that great inner pool of divine affluence.

After a while the experience of finding and dwelling in that safe place in spirit becomes contagious. To be in the presence of a person who is identified with that light, with that safe place, is to be present within a field of consciousness that arouses within all those nearby a corresponding consciousness.

Remember this: consciousness is an energy, and a new form of energy can be induced into any state of consciousness. It is similar to electricity. Repeated inductions will finally arouse sympathetic pulsations. An individual thus exposed to another's illumined consciousness for the first time becomes established in his own safe place in spirit. He becomes one, grounded in the higher knowledge, instead of being a mere student on the way. He seizes every possible opportunity to come within the sphere of his own divine light and to achieve greater and greater realizations of that divine light. He discovers that all the many other facets of himself are interrelated with that safe place. He is awakened.

Achieving the safe place in spirit means learning

how to integrate (while still embodied) the outer and the inner levels of being. With this integration there comes a fusion, and the continual presence of that fusion between the personality and the soul results in oneness.

There are several basic realizations needed in order to establish permanently the safe place in spirit. First, you must be able to say to yourself, "I am only God. God is not something other than I. I am only God." Secondly, you must realize, "I am only knowledge. Knowledge is not separate from me. In the safe place in spirit knowledge and I are one."

At the crucial moment of the realization of the safe place in spirit, there is a very deep feeling of calmness. Something very deep and very strong takes hold inwardly, and forever after the activity and the events previously centered in the personal consciousness cease to have any power. In the deepest part of the being then life is totally free, and that freedom is continuously reflected in the outer life.

There comes a time when every individual must turn his back upon the outer aspect of life and turn within. Otherwise he can expect a barren and unfruitful existence. This step involves for a brief period a certain giving over to inward quietness and the acceptance, "Nothing else matters." Attachment to lesser values is a barrier to the realization of the greater value of the safe place in spirit.

The individual wins power in every direction by concentration upon the safe place in spirit. It is necessary to suppress outside activity, at least for certain periods within the life pattern. Main interests in life are continued, but all incidental peripheral interests fall away. If the main interest in a man's life is so all-consuming that there hardly remains any conflicting interest or desire, it may well be that he is on the road to enlightenment. In any case, mastery in any field, including the field of spirit, requires discipline. Let the individual concentrate his full effort upon that which he desires most to have accomplished in his life, and let him restrain or transform incompatible desires. Those things that in reality have no meaning to the greater life then fall away.

Always, as you seek the safe place in spirit, there will be temptations in the outer world. Do not dodge temptation. Face it until it is mastered. Cultivate within yourself the act of conscientious application to duty. Yet combine that conscientiousness with a kind of impersonalization, a detachment from the situation at hand. Strength is preferable to weakness. The safe place in spirit is preferable to the external world of illusion.

Once you are grounded in the safe place in spirit, there is a tendency for your inner nature to unfold towards balance so that finally you reach a point that is symbolized by the great eagle with two wings equally strong. These two wings are compassion and intelligence.

What do you do then from the safe place in spirit? First and foremost, you dwell there in serenity. Having fully established your capacity to dwell in the safe place in spirit, you look not to right nor to left but straight forward and you say, "What, oh Father, do you wish of me from this safe place that you have so kindly provided for me?" Then you wait. And for what do you wait? For motion, a motion that comes from within. Motion in the highest sense is spontaneous and does not have to be explained. You do not have to say, "What shall I do?" or "How shall I do it?" You wait from that safe place in spirit for the inner impulse that will lead you to uplifting concepts and inspirational ideas concerning this world of matter.

Anyone who has ever dwelt, even for a brief time, in the safe place in spirit will know that it does not imply the cessation of activity on the outer level. It is indeed a place quite different from anything to be found within the outer field, the field of relativity. Approaching your whole life from the safe place in spirit, you are like a point in space. And in that space you have a vision of what to do.

Sensation of motion precedes manifestation and is the foundation upon which all manifestation rests. From the safe place in spirit you will no longer need to be careful of your moods or emotions, for there will be an unbroken connection between the safe place and your external world. From the safe place in spirit you will be able to realize the folly of your past experiences, and you will have no desire whatsoever to repeat that folly. The opinions of others will no longer endure as a basis from which to function. You will look with quiet solicitude upon the ramblings and the discomforts of others. You will offer them a blessing, and you will say in your silent breath, "May God bring them forth to that safe place in spirit which I have found." You will not need to proselytize. You will not need to tell others of the place that you have found, for it will be evident by your very presence.

You will begin to find, from that safe place in spirit, your true ministry in the field of God's action. For remember: the only purpose of life on Earth in human form is the manifestation of God realized. The soil of all the centuries has been cultivated for the gospel of God. But that gospel has been overlooked because men have become so immersed in outer world activity that they have forgotten that it is in God's heart that the safe place exists. A worker in God's field is known by his influence upon his environment and by the degree to which he can maintain inner stability as he develops an ever widening scope of service to the world.

The world is in need of those people who have learned from the secret of their hearts the key to the safe place in spirit. All too soon will come the new age energy. Even now it is being felt in every corner of the known universe. As this energy emerges and begins to fill the consciousness of man with the new way, the way of light, the old order must pass away. Founders in the new order will be those who have discovered the safe place in spirit and who continuously dwell therein.

Chapter Fourteen
Silence, Solitude and the Great Planetary Wind Chamber

We will now consider the subject of silence and solitude.

Silence usually implies the complete absence of sound, particularly sound of an external nature. In the development of an advanced spiritual life, silence is abstinence from unnecessary speech, stopping the activity of the mind, and putting to rest all unnecessary preoccupation with thought. Solitude is being alone, retiring from all external activities, withdrawing from all external events.

Can you not see how the two go in hand? Ambiguity occurs when the aspirant elects to enter into the silence and to develop the capacity for solitude but then allows intercepting forces to pull him away from his planned course of action. For example, it is ambiguous to decide to settle into a period of four to eight hours of silence and solitude and then to neglect to detach oneself from the world. It would be ambiguous to set up a course of action of silence and solitude and then invite a friend for dinner.

In the midst of the very demanding life that most men and women of modern society have, the necessity of regular periods of silence and solitude cannot be over-emphasized. You can develop such a deep capacity for silence and solitude that even in the heart of a city you can literally close out all external stimuli. You can project such a powerful tube of light and power around yourself that even a great storm thundering in the heavens would not be heard or experienced. Obviously, this ability calls for regular practice and for an intense, disciplined concentration.

The difference between the concepts of silence and solitude and the study of meditation is significant. In the act of establishing for yourself — for your growth — silence and solitude, you do not stop activity. You simply detach yourself from all sound through an act of will and establish solitude by creating around yourself the winds of the cosmos, which whirl about you with such mighty power that it is as if you are in the eye of the cyclone. Then, in that center of power you do whatever you wish, whether it is to read a philosophical treatise, to work upon your own writings, to raise your consciousness upward and commune with the power of other dimensions, or simply to dwell there as you move about doing chosen tasks.

You will find, once you master the art of silence and solitude, that the power that you build in conscious expression will generate within you a new octave, a greater capacity for the process we call thinking. The process of thinking is entirely different from thought preoccupation. Thinking from a center of silence and solitude can bring about instantaneous results.

Let us take an example. Say that you have a particular subject to pursue, such as philosophy. Let us narrow that subject to, say, the philosophy of Kant and further limit it to Kant's commentary on reason. Once you have entered the vortex of silence, your place of solitude, take the works of Kant on the subject of reason, read them, and then put the book down, and in a fully conscious state enter the domain of Kant and dwell there and exchange ideas with him. Having exchanged ideas with him, you then can transmit those ideas into your own understanding and incorporate them into your own philosophy of life. The process is so totally different from "studying Kant" that there is absolutely no comparison of the two.

Silence does not necessarily mean an absence of inner sound, for you may, when you enter the silence and establish your solitude, hear the great sound of the spheres. You may hear the high notes of the greater worlds. If you engage yourself in silence and solitude with regularity you will find that you are linked to realms of realization of which you have no concept in your ordinary life or even in the life of meditation.

There is a place in the cosmos of your planetary system where a great "wind chamber" exists. It is, in a way, a rejuvenation chamber, and it is entered through the silence of the soul. Up to now we have talked about the silence and the solitude of your third dimensional world, from which you can enter the fourth dimensional world — and even higher dimensions. When we speak of the great wind chamber, we are speaking of the silence of another world. You move through a series of locks. As you go into the chamber of each lock you drop particles of your nature that have no place in the great inner chamber. Because of the refining process that takes place as you go through the seven locks, when you finally enter the great chamber you are in your pure light body.

Others may be in the great chamber at the same time, but because of your own vortex of power you will not experience them — except as a misty impression. You may walk around the great chamber, or you may stand with your hands raised to the power of the cosmic wind. You will not want to stay long, for if you stayed too long, you would forget all too readily that you have a physical body that awaits you. Angelic attendants keep watch. If they see that you are tempted to linger too long, they touch you lightly and escort you out through the locks, the seven locks, through which you entered.

From a slightly different perspective consider the "wind chamber" as a powerful funnel of light, whirling energy moved by cosmic wind. Imagine, as you are outside of that funnel of light, that you see an opening into the funnel. You stand before the funnel; it is whirling in great motion, and you see an opening by which you may enter. You walk through. Immediately after you enter, the opening behind you closes, and you stand in that great funnel of cosmic light and wind.

At first your head swims and you feel overpowered with so much dynamic energy that you think you can hardly stand the pressure. But since you have made your entrance into this cosmic tunnel of power, you determine to stay. Soon the pressure upon your head lightens. Finally it goes away altogether, and you feel a sensation of great orgasmic power bursting through your head, filling every particle of your brain with light.

As you accept this immersion in light, you realize the infinite potential of your own capacity to unite with Supreme Cosmic Infinite Intelligence. Having thus entered the vortex of power, the great funnel of the universe, you then move about in your own environment, doing whatever you would do, knowing every moment that you are in this powerful energy component. You have created this energy component of your own volition by establishing silence and solitude.

Illumination can only come to the aspiring heart through deliberate entrance into the contemplative state of silence and solitude. It is true, illumination comes to some at unexpected moments. But if an investigation were made it would show that those unexpected moments were brought about through the entrance of the awareness into a state of silence and solitude.

Once you have worked with diligence and discipline to bring into your consciousness the realization of the meaning of silence and solitude, you will be able to key in, to enter into that state of being, at the flickering of an eyelid, whether you are in the midst of a great hustle of activity or alone upon the mountain top.

The simplicity of the meaning of silence and

solitude is such that it is nearly impossible to convey the fullness of the meaning. For in attempting to convey the fullness, we must use words. As you develop and become more aware of this powerful understanding, you will begin to realize the nature of the word and the nature of the meaning of the interval between words. You will seek the interval at the end of the breath and incorporate it into your understanding of silence and solitude. For it is a good thing to discover that at that tiniest of moments, at the end of exhalation, there is absolute silence and solitude, which is the vacuum from which everything manifests. Man can force a period of silence as he inhales, but he cannot generally experience silence and solitude at the peak of inhalation. That experience comes at the end of the exhalation.

There are many secrets in the great universe. When the student aspires, through purification of his vehicle, he is given glimpses of a world beyond this world. Interestingly enough, all of these cosmic revelations have significantly more meaning when they are experienced through the densest of matter, which is one of the reasons individuals of high evolvement choose to incarnate on Earth. Earth provides the greatest potential for contrast and thus for the realization of the cosmic revelation. Souls of high evolvement, particularly those souls who have dwelt on the Earth many, many times in order to assist the evolution of Earth, gather the depth of the universe into their bosom while in physical incarnation, experiencing and tasting and sensing and realizing it all. And eventually, after eons of such exposure, they return to their homeland in the heart of God.

In the modern world the fact that even a few people are willing to develop the art of dwelling in the silence and experiencing solitude is quite miraculous. Yet as the age before you unfolds, more and more will seek this knowledge of how to enter the silence, and the nature of the benefits of the dominion of silence. You will not be able to teach them unless you have dwelt there yourself.

Chapter Fifteen
Destiny and Life Design

According to the way you design your life, you create your destiny. Let us for a few moments examine the meaning of the word *design*. A design is an original creation, which comes from contemplating what you wish to create. A design is a pattern by which you can bring about a creation. Without a design, a life is often lived without rhyme or reason, without purpose or intent.

Man would benefit much by teaching his children in their early years a simple method for designing their lives. The ancients did this. When a child was born the astrologers were called in to confer, and the design of the life was carefully presented to the parents. Thus the indications were already at hand when the infant became a child. And at a very early age the child was presented with the possibilities open to him, according to those astrological configurations under which he was born. He was given a name in accordance with his destiny, his design. And he began to have, at a very early age, a realization of his life purpose

— whether the child was to become a worker in a rice paddy, a physician, a seer, or a tool maker.

In time modernization came about, and this concept was lost. Most of the people born upon the planet today wander aimlessly about using as their only method of discerning the design of their lives that element called chance. Upon rare occasion you find an integrated man who knows that he has the capacity to become a writer, a musician, a poet, a scientist, a diplomat, or whatever.

When a person discovers a need for the redesign of his life, he can begin at once — no matter where he is or what he is doing. He can at any point make a thorough inquiry into *who* he is, right where he is — his interests, his drives, his motivation, his inner longing — and begin to create a life design for himself. He can call upon the various elements in his own inner nature to find his strengths and his weaknesses, and he can begin from that point to draw upon his strengths and to minimize his weaknesses, to educate himself in ways of using those strengths and to forego indulgence in the weaknesses.

It is a matter of clearly discerning the nature of your being, of seeing what capacities you have and what you can draw forth to meet life in a happy, free, and joyous way. Once an individual has decided upon a plan for his life design, he begins to attract every attribute for the fulfillment of that life design. He finds in the inner recesses of his being attributes that he did not know existed. If he wishes to become, let us say, a successful scientist, and he has never realized before his capacity for logic, when he begins to study science that capacity for logic will come forth. It was latent within him, waiting for him to draw upon it and bring it into full manifestation. There is no attribute that a man could possibly need that is not latent within him. The fact that he had a desire to use that attribute is an indication that it is, indeed, latent within him.

Once the life design has been brought forth, once the person desires to do thus and so, whatever it happens to be, all avenues will open to enable him to achieve his goal. The life design must come before destiny starts unfolding.

A man can have many talents. A man may be capable of building a great edifice and at the same time expressing himself as a poet. So his life design would allow room in his daily experience for expressing both the life of the architect and the life of the poet. Thus his design becomes more intricate. He may, at some point in his evolution in a given life, see that he wishes to add another dimension to his life — say , music. Most men, when they realize they have such a desire, will wave the idea aside as being whimsical. In fact, for a man to add the new dimension of music to his life would enrich each of the other areas of his life. It would enhance his capacity as an architect and his capacity as a poet.

So in the life design you see that you will be utilizing many threads and colors. You will be selective in choosing the right color and the right strength of thread, and the quantity of each color that you wish to weave into the life design.

The idea begins with knowing that you are worthwhile. The life design cannot be created until you begin with an understanding of yourself, recognize that each and every attribute that you were born with is worthwhile, and start to minimize your weaknesses, fortify your strengths and bring them forth.

When a man finds that he is, let us say, adept at foretelling the weather, then he seeks a way to enhance that natural talent. He educates himself in every area that has to do with his subject. He leaves no stone unturned in finding all bits of information that will enable him to be the finest weatherman. If a man desires to be a minister to the people, he begins by examining those attributes that he may already have within his own being that would be useful in that profession. He then enhances them through education so that he can make optimum use of his talents.

Desire is indeed the word of God speaking to the individual. If he has a desire to serve as a minister or as a diplomat or as a linguist, then he has inherent within him the qualities endowed by his Creator for accomplishing his goal.

The life design could be compared to a mural that a great artist would paint upon a wall. First, he conceptualizes what he wishes to portray. Perhaps he makes numerous sketches of the idea. He indicates upon his sketches where the different colors will be — the pastels, the deep colors, the darker tones, the lighter tones. Having satisfied himself with the idea outlined on his sketching pad, he collects his supplies, all the various tubes of paint, the brushes, the cleansers, the washes. He studies carefully the many sketches that he has made. He alters a bit here, a bit there. Finally he is satisfied that he has upon his sketch pad all that he envisioned the mural to be.

The next thing that he does is scale the mural. He lays it out with care. He indicates where every figure will appear and the size it will be. Having laid out the mural and sectioned it in, he begins to apply the paint. His destiny as an artist is to paint a great mural, but he could not have painted it without first creating the design. Thus it is with life.

The true destiny of any man is to create a great mural of his life, whether it be the simple life of the farmer who tends the field or the greatness of the composer who creates a symphony. First, he sketches out what he wants his life to be, what his inner voice tells him, then he fills in the spaces, carefully. Every idea that he has ever had about himself must be taken into consideration. Finally he has a clear picture of his life design, and that, when incorporated into his daily use of energy, becomes his destiny.

Questioning yourself, moment by moment, taking time to write upon your sketch pad, to erase, to revise, to clarify, to project, is the most rewarding thing that you as an incarnated person can do for yourself. Life is not to be lived accidentally and incidentally. Life is to be lived with care. Each individual born into any given life is most fortunate to have been given the breath of life. Though he be given not, upon his birth, a map, though he be given not a book of instructions, he nevertheless has the most priceless of all gifts — the breath of life. The parents of the child look at the infant and wonder what he will be, what he will become. And yet all too often they fail to make deep inquiry into the potential of their child. And so the child grows, enters school, and begins the long process of being prepared for life by those who know him not.

At some point, perhaps he begins to get a glimmering of what he would like to do with the life he has been given, but all too often by the time he reaches maturity he has been so infused with society's plan for him that he never sees the light of his own plan. And this indeed is a sadness.

Parents can change this somewhat by early contemplation with the masters of astrology and the masters of evolution. Though it is not likely that this approach will be popular for the present generation, it is possible that future generations will once again consult the stars for the indications of a reborn's destiny. Any individual at any age can begin the same type of consultation for himself and draw for himself insights of a profound nature. He can sit in the quiet of his own being and ask the question, "What am I to do here now that I am here?" And if he is quiet and asks the question deeply enough he will hear the answer. He will then begin to create a life design that will lead to his greater destiny.

It becomes evident that those who do not, at some point in their use of the life breath, look for and begin to create the idea of their life design may have no destiny. For destiny is an earned point, earned by individual effort towards self-understanding. Those who do not create a life design for themselves end up with what we commonly call "their own fate". Whatever they set in motion, whether it be accidental or incidental, leads them to a kind of ill-fated end, or an end that has no meaning.

So the creation of the life design is of great importance. The creation of the life design leads to ultimate destiny. The noncreation of the life design leads to a fate of anonymity, often to a fate of pain and sorrow. The emphasis then is this: for parents to look upon their newborn one and say, "I have a responsibility to give this infant guidelines and indications of its life design."

The individual who has not had such good fortune (and such of course is the case for the majority) must listen to his heart, to his inner mind, for the guidance that will give him an indication of what his life design should be. Having listened carefully, he acts upon the information that he has heard and begins immediately to create his own life design — his destiny.

Chapter Sixteen
Ultimate Individuality

It is essential that seekers of the path cease to labor under the misconception that they must give up their individuality for the group. This is nonsense! Never was it intended for an individual to sublimate his individuality to the group; rather, the individual is to be a dynamic, integral part of the group.

Ultimate Individuality is a statement that though you may serve with diligence and dedication the great hierarchial plan, you do not need to bury your individuality. Ultimate Individuality requires that you study your individuality as a part of the greater whole and that you realize that without the perfection of the individuality, the greater whole would be less than perfect in its perfection.

And so, having taken this approach, you begin to look at all the aspects of your inner and outer reality that are *unique to you.* You cannot say that it is unique to have two hands, two eyes, one nose, two feet, two knees, and so on, for these characteristics are unique only to the race called humanity.

But you can say, as an individualized expression of the greater God Being, "I have these unique characteristics and qualities, and I can expand and perfect these qualities, which I find through self-investigation and self-inquiry. I can deepen these qualities, increase these qualities, and make them a part of the expansion of the greater universe of my being. Thus I, through this ultimate perfection of my individuality, contribute to the greater oneness of the universe." This is a single but profound concept and one that will bear much consideration as you work into your new octave of consciousness.

The second universal concept is this: "Around and about me I see the *myriad expressions of Infinity.* I select various parts of these expressions, and I study them. Just as a scientist studies slides under a microscope, I take these individualized levels of consciousness, whether they be in the mineral, the animal, the vegetable, or the human kingdom; I study them, and I say to myself, 'What do I see here that can increase my awareness of the greater universality of Being, which is all about me?'" And thus you study all of life.

The third universal concept is this: "All through the kingdom of humanity there is running a *golden thread of light,* which is invisible to my ordinary vision but which is visible to my higher consciousness. To that other level of my awareness, there is that golden thread that runs through and connects every single person that is born into the human kingdom." We speak here not of the other kingdoms, but of the human kingdom. And as you see this golden thread of light weaving its way through every single mind, through the brain of every human being on Earth, you begin to sense the wonder of it all. You begin to see the connectedness that cannot be broken. You then realize that if the man in the slums of India suffers a swollen gland or a broken limb, every other member of humanity suffers it also. You bring this realization into conscious awareness, and everything about you in the human kingdom takes on a new meaning.

Having considered these three major universal concepts (ultimate individuality, myriad expressions of Infinity, and the golden thread), you begin to see the relatedness of the three and to develop and unfold a philosophy of life that is useful in extending and expanding your own consciousness as you go toward that ultimate of all goals — mastery in the universal sense.

And so, from where you stand in your universal reality, in the cosmic sense of being, you are as essential in the overall evolution of the universe as is the "top man on the totem pole", and you are as essential as is the new soul.

Let us say, for example, that the one flaw that exists in your being, which you have carried over many, many lifetimes, is your tendency to be judgmental. Once you have ferreted this fault out, captured it, and removed it totally from your consciousness, you will have accomplished the ultimate mastery, which you designed this particular life to accomplish.

You saw this major flaw in your being long before you planned this present incarnation. You knew that it was there long before you discussed it with your teachers, the elder ones who have traveled the way with you, and you agreed that you would take one whole lifetime in which to work through this major flaw, which kept you from attaining perfect consciousness. And you have diligently worked upon this from time to time — frequently, in fact. But like the little creature that burrows into the ground and hides for fear of the light, this flaw burrows into the deeper stratas of your personality, hides there, and waits until you turn your attention away. Then it darts out again and begins once more to control your personality.

There are many ways of capturing this demon residing within you. I hasten to tell you, dedicated ones of the Light, that everyone, no matter how powerful their station in physical embodiment, has at least one of these little demons to capture, so you are not alone. The great way is the simple way. It is to say, "I see this demon within me, and I will take it out and make it into my domesticated pet. And once having won it to be my little domesticated pet then I will charge it with the responsibility of total transformation until it will cease to be my enemy and will become my friend."

But first one must capture the little scurrying creature, tame it, and domesticate it. Eventually it will go through total transformation and will be, instead of an enemy who works against you, a friend who works with you. Judgmentalism will turn into discernment. Discernment is revealing insight and understanding, a characteristic to be cultivated.

Achievement of ultimate individuality requires the refinement of all attributes within the personality vehicle. We have looked at the attribute of judgmentalism and shown how it can be refined into discernment. Just so, any negative tendency can be refined and experienced as a positive tendency. Without this process of refinement, ultimate individuality would not be achieved.

Part Four
Passing
The Torch

Chapter Seventeen
Preparation for the New World Order

Universes and worlds are built through cyclic manifestations. Throughout all time the Creator has expressed cyclically. We will discuss the nature of cyclical evolution pertaining to planet Earth and its inhabitants.

At the origin of Earth, chaos reigned for millions of years. The nature of such chaos is that it is nonmanifested. Out of the nonmanifest came, over eons of time, the manifest, and that manifest formed itself into various expressions. Archaeology and history will quickly reveal the multitude of manifestations that the Creator set into energetic motion. Prehistoric days revealed entirely different manifestations than modern days. We are particularly concerned here with the nature of modern day change.

All about you are seen the results of man's failing to grow according to Divine Plan. Devastating experiences come upon all those whose crystallized forms of consciousness have remained intact. Though these people have been given numerous opportunities for evolution, they have remained in virtually the same state of consciousness.

Evident everywhere upon the planet today are signs that the old world order is breaking down. This development is in keeping with the cyclic nature of the evolution of the planet. It seems necessary for destruction to take place, leaving chaos in its wake, before the new world order can emerge. Destruction, as you can see in this cycle of time, is everywhere to behold.

The old world order consists of persons who have come from various areas of evolution, where they have developed various forms of crystallized patterns and where they have not grown, except in a miniscule degree. These waves of humanity comprise millions of people who in other cycles of time did not achieve any degree of God awareness and who collected themselves together almost as an animalistic group spirit and made yet another sojourn into physical manifestation for the era at hand. Millions of these people are undergoing extremely traumatic evolutionary processes in order that they may realize the nature of God and turn to their Creator.

It is difficult for many incarnated souls not to feel compassion for these people because another sector of humanity has evolved so rapidly and developed a sympathetic nature for all living life. In the transfer of souls from one level of consciousness to another, the plan provides that those of higher evolution will look after their younger brothers as they enter into the collapse of their particular level of evolution.

So you see in the world today the preparation for a new world order, which is the destruction of all the various levels of the old world order characterized by greed, avarice, ignorance, and the stupidity revealed in all forms of human degradation, such as improper housing and starvation. All of these manifestations are easy to behold upon Earth today. Thus those who have throughout eons of time developed the higher states of consciousness turn all attention at this time towards preparing themselves for greater and greater tasks in establishing the new world order.

The multitudes who exit through various cataclysmic events — flood, storm, isolation, deprivation — reenter over and over again, and they must be taken care of in some humane way. For the new world order it is necessary to prepare hundreds of thousands of souls who will be humanitarians, who will care, teach, uplift, and express concern. They will be the statesmen, the physicians, the nurses, the teachers, the administrators, the healers, and the inventors. These servers begin to realize the imperative of world unity and of the development of a "caring process" so that no speck of humanity can resist the pull to the higher life.

In preparation for the new world order, the first thing that must happen is the establishment of the caring process by those of the higher nature, so that universal caring can take place. Thus concern for feeding the world will be well established, for empty bellies leave little time for conscious evolution. Although all of those affected are experiencing their plight from their own level of consciousness, in the new world order that level of conciousness can be changed in many by the caring process.

How can those in crystallized consciousness of fear and deprivation turn their hearts and minds toward God when their bellies are collapsing from hunger? How can a mother believe that there is a God when her baby is dying in her arms because her breasts can no longer nourish it? How can the man who has fourteen children to feed, and who can only eke out a meager living, believe that God exists?

There are in the present stage of Earth's development millions of people who are leaving their countries because they have experienced nothing but the worst form of degradation. The United States and other nations around the world have formulated a plan for taking hundreds of thousands of these people in. This plan is erroneous for the most part, for it is extremely disorienting to the stability of a country to take in more than a certain number of immigrants. It would be far wiser to make preparation to give boundless quantities of assistance in the form of warm clothing, food, and shelter, to those people in the various nations where they now reside.

The United States of America is uniquely equipped to propose such a plan through the United Nations. The hierarchy, consisting of the elder ones of the race, is attempting to interpenetrate the consciousness of senators and world statesmen to turn attention toward feeding the starving millions where they are rather than causing their disorientation by moving them to a strange land.

Preparation for the new world order involves three stages — feeding, teaching, and finally *freeing*. For it does no good to feed and teach unless you also *free* the individuals.

The new world order is already formulated on the higher dimensional levels. It indeed calls for the inauguration of a golden age of awareness. Many millions of souls are being prepared to incarnate to assist in this process of establishing the new world order. So you have a balancing. In order to counterbalance the millions who come and go in the lesser countries, where technology has not been developed for feeding and teaching as a basis for evolutionary growth, you have a great number of persons attempting to come to Earth to create the concept of world unity based upon the three stages just delineated.

The new world order also will be characterized by a deeper and fuller communication between worlds, which involves recognition of the process called "channeling" as a valid means of communication when in the care of an appropriate, well-trained instrument, the channel. (See Part Two, "Communication with Other Dimensions.") Also, visibility between worlds will develop so that the hundreds of thousands of people who have stepped upon the path of light while in physical embodiment will be able to see and hear (aside from the process of channeling) those of higher dimensional awareness who work with them in the world.

The individual preparing for his role in the new world order faces the necessity of making certain simple decisions:

I desire to serve: I will *serve.*

I will cleanse myself of the lower emotional body so that it ceases to have any control over my life. I recognize that the lower emotional body is a creation of human-ness, that it has no reality, nothing to do with my angelic self. Therefore, I will cleanse myself of that body and transmute those feelings, which formerly were filled with emotionalism, into the higher feeling body.

I will be alert and aware of the needs of my fellow man. I will not interfere when the hand upon my shoulder says to leave something alone, but when the thought in my inner awareness is to assist, I will do so. I will develop great keenness in the power of discernment so that I will know where I am to serve and where I am to leave things alone.

I will pray and I will meditate and I will contemplate the wonders of the world, the wonders of my association with like beings, and the wonder of my association with God.

I will look about me and ascertain the most perfect place that I can be upon the planet Earth from which my work can be done. I will willingly remove myself from conditions that appear to be desolate, confused, or difficult, knowing that from the point of view of my energy system I cannot afford as a worker on the path of light to go down into the lower elements. In order that my light may shine brightly, I will remove myself from all lower elements of humanity, blessing them from a distance, but not partaking of their confusion.

I will with great regularity realize my dominion

over my physical world. I will realize it so thoroughly that my physical world eventually merges totally with my higher world. I will at times clearly realize my whereness, *knowing that if I insist upon being merely human, I will be coated with the human world, but if I remember to be one with my angelic self, I will be lifted constantly and continuously into that angelic self.*

It is possible, as the new world order emerges, to realize one's immortality. (See Chapter 7, "Immortality.") Death is not necessary, except as it is willed by the soul once the life work is complete. It is not necessary to make and remake, make and remake, bodies. It is possible through diligent application of spiritual knowledge to maintain any given physical vehicle for an extended time. Since the new world order is emerging even now and will be, if all goes as planned by the elder ones, fully established by the year 2010, it behooves those who are interested in service to the new world order, who are physically embodied at the present time, to care with great concern and eager interest for the physical vehicle, according to their own divine guidance. It is not necessary to have this authority or that authority tell you what to do to care for your vehicle; your vehicle will tell you itself. It knows what is right for you and what is not right. It knows what food it needs and what food it does not need, and if you follow the continuous feedback that you receive from your own vehicle, you may sustain the life energy for as long as you desire. Remember too that correct attitudes are also important for sustaining the physical vehicle.

There is no reason to be subject to accidents, sickness, or pain — except as pain is a warning factor that something may be wrong. It is possible to maintain with full vitality a vehicle that is in fairly reasonable shape at the time the decision for long-term maintenance is made. It is possible to rejuvenate that vehicle and maintain it for as long as the individual desires, which can be hundreds of years, without aging, maintaining the perfect expression of physical reality.

The actual nature of the new world order cannot be clearly defined yet, for it is undergoing its own evolution, and its more subtle characteristics are as yet unknown. Its main characteristic will be world unity, caring, the diligent effort to eliminate degradation among all people and the establishment of intelligent and wise community action on a world basis. The new world order will see the reappearance of great statesmen who have been absent for a long time working on the inner level. The new world order will see the return of certain avatars. (See "The Way of the Avatar", page 119.)

The individual must realize that his particular role in the new world order is to maintain the integrity of all levels of his being. This process is simple, yet even those on the path have a tendency to complicate it. Here is the simple method for maintaining integrity on all levels:

First, evaluate in a simple and direct way what you consider to be your personal integrity. Evaluate that integrity on all levels, physical, mental, feeling, and spiritual. Be clear about your concept of personal integrity. Ask yourself, "What is this to me?

What does this event, act, or thought mean to me?" Let every aspect of life meet the requirements of your personal integrity, without deviation. Second, if an individual who is stepping deeply into the consciousness of the new world order is unclear about his role, let him seek counsel, for already there are those avatars of light upon the Earth who are willing, even eager, to help.

As for the role of personages not in physical embodiment who dwell in the fourth dimension, they are ever about you, willing and eager to serve. Yet if you will not hear them they cannot serve except through the transfer of spiritual energy from one domain to another. That is the subject of another commentary. Let it be sufficient now to say they are one with you, they serve you, they are here.

Chapter Eighteen
Responsibility of the Individual in Prevailing World Conditions

Now to discuss briefly the responsibility of the individual in prevailing world conditions.

First, let us describe the nature of prevailing world conditions.

Due to developments in modern communications, it is possible to pick up clear information broadcast on the ether waves, enabling almost instantaneous reporting. So it is possible to know prevailing world conditions through the media. For example, you know at this time that in one country there has been a major revolution. In another country there has been a catastrophic earthquake. In another place, a war is going on; in another a volcano has erupted; elsewhere a famine is occurring.

The question then arises, what can the individual do in the midst of prevailing world conditions? What can the individual do, for example, about the animosity of one group of men toward another? What can an individual do about a flood? What can an individual do in the presence of the dire catastrophic experiences of war? What can the individual who is walking upon the path of light, who has sought the way of inner development, do to make it possible for that energy factor, that power factor, which he has built into his being, to be utilized for the benefit of the world?

First, do this: pray without ceasing, as the Lord Christ once admonished his disciples. He said, "Go ye among all of the people of the world, and as ye go forth be certain that ye pray without ceasing."

This concept is almost incomprehensible to modern man, even though he may be in the process of becoming an esoteric student, a disciple of the way. For how can one perform one's daily chores, meet the demands made upon one, arising at an early hour and working until late at night, and have the time to pray without ceasing?

Here is the key. Prayer, once realized as a *process of awareness,* not something to do, can go on in the midst of all external activity.

The line to remember and maintain within your consciousness, regardless of what distracting circumstances may surround you, is this: *"I am the Resurrection and the Life."*

This line was chosen appropriately at the time when the Christian world was celebrating the resurrection of the Christ from the tomb into the ascension. Constant repetition of the line instills within you that conviction that you are the light, the ascending life, the salvation of the world.

Take also the line, *"There is only God."* Let this be your prayer. So thoroughly implant the line into your awareness that it is a continuous remembrance, regardless of what is going on in the external world.

Thus you will begin to experience prayer without ceasing.

A second condition for prayer without ceasing is to develop the capacity for ultimate compassion in all situations. Imagine yourself and the image of a starving man standing on a street corner. There is chaos on the street and you are safe in your car. With some risk to you, you stop the car, walk to the starving man, and give him coin and paper money, saying, "Go and get some food for yourself." Then you put your hand upon his shoulder, bless him, and return to the car and go on your way.

Repeat this image often and in your heart will develop a compassion that will reach beyond your small world to India, China, wherever people are in need.

A third action is to gather about individuals of like mind who wish to become a part of a vocalized unit for power. This group would be a focus for great energy, to work invisibly, with great sensitivity, for order and peace within prevailing world conditions.

This is an extension of an experiment begun in 1875, which was continued in another form in 1935, and activated again in 1955, at which time certain teachers of higher dimensions prepared channels to receive philosophical and educational material from a particular group of teachers. The experiments have been sufficiently satisfactory that it is appropriate to continue them.

These, then, are the three individual actions to perform in the midst of prevailing world conditions:

- Pray without ceasing.
- Develop the capacity for ultimate compassion in all situations.
- Become a part of a group unit of power.

While the action of bringing about cooperation and understanding is going on, there must also be the decrystallization of crystalized forms of consciousness, which have existed for long periods of time. Masses of people who have been locked into this fixed consciousness bring about catastrophes. Catastrophies are not created by God. They are created by the consciousness of man.

Let us begin now to search for further ideas on how the individual can be effective in prevailing world conditions, keeping in mind that he can indeed enhance his own evolution while being thus effective.

The Way of the Avatar

One of the Ancient Ones stood upon a plateau high up on a mountain top looking out across the world spread before him in all its shimmering light. In his left hand he held a long stick, and in his right he cupped a bird about to take flight. The bird trembled, turning its tiny bright eye toward him as though awaiting an instruction. Finally the Old One leaned down and whispered a word to the bird. Then with a little toss he released it to the heavens. As the bird flew over the Earth it grew, its wing span became enormous, and finally, as it flew away into the distance, it changed from a bird into an angel.

The Old One watched as the angel took flight. His eyes glistened, and his heart pulsated with gladness, for lo, another angel had been sent to Earth. But the mystery of the word the Old One spoke to the bird remained unsolved.

The angel soared across the heavens, making a gradual descent down through the lights, which shone in all their splendor over various parts of the world. Occasionally he would soar to the left or to the right, but always he descended closer and closer to the physical Earth. He noticed, as he made his descent, that the lower he went the less light there was. And he longed in his heart to return to the mountain splendor. But the word had been spoken — the angel must go forth.

Lower and lower he flew until finally there was no light except a faint glimmer of the light he had left. He noticed below him a mighty metropolis. He heard the hum of millions of voices on the ether waves. He felt his body beginning to thicken, his wings beginning to diminish, and his size becoming smaller and smaller until finally he was a bird again. And he found himself alighting upon the rooftop of a great building. On the ether waves he heard that the building was called a skyscraper. He wondered why he was there, for he had forgotten the word given by the Old One on the shining mountain top.

He fluttered his wings and wondered how he could depart from the skyscraper and go back to the shining mountain. But he knew that his wings were too weak to carry him there and that he would have to stay where he was. He thought, "Perhaps it will be better if I fly lower." He looked below him, and his head seemed to swim. He wondered whether he could make any further descent without destroying himself.

Finally he decided, instinctively, to fly to the very Earth itself. And so he began, fluttering and flapping his wings, going down, down, down. As he descended to the pavement he found himself startled to be a bird walking among the legs and feet of men. In this moment of utter alarm, he ruffled feathers and longed for his return. And as he was longing, the transformation from a bird into a man took place. He walked among the people and wondered, "What am I to do here?" and finally his inner ear recalled the word that the Old One had spoken before he took flight, *"Avatar, avatar, go the way of the avatar."*

But the word had no meaning to him. He was perplexed and confused by the body that he inhabited. *Avatar.* He stopped someone who was walking beside him. He seemed to know their language and he said to the man, "Do you know what 'avatar' means?" The man looked at him perplexed. "No, I don't," he said and walked busily on down the street. Again and again he stopped and asked this person and that person, "What means 'avatar'?" No one could reply.

Finally one kind woman, seeing his perplexity, said, "Why don't you go to the library. It's only down the street a ways. They can surely tell you there what the word 'avatar' means."

He thanked the lady and walked where she had directed. Going into the library he met a kindly woman who said, "No, I don't know what it means, but we can look it up."

Together they stood in front of a great book of words, which rested on a pedestal, and looked in the *A's*, and finally as the woman ran her finger down the page, she found with him and for him the meaning of the word.

He turned and left the library and has been walking the Earth ever since, discovering for himself the way of the avatar.

Appendix-Summary

Summary of Guidance provided in Krishanta and the Way of the Avatar

PART ONE. POWER, LIGHT, ENERGY

1. Power — the Golden Key

   Be aware of your own power. It is the Golden Key.

   Dwell on power: through knowing, through kindness, through strength, through determination.

   Invoke the power of the healing Christ in every moment.

   Express power over your own being.

   Pass courageously through the burning ground. Let old habits, old conditions be buried.

   Remove the veil from your eyes through prayer, decree, meditation, dedication.

   Be alert to the powers that work with you.

2. The Inner Sun and the Torch

   First, know the inner light through meditation, through focused attention. By deliberate design bring it forth into daily activity.

   Gain the light also by humility, through asking the sun to

penetrate mind, body, spirit.

Focus the inner light to a pinpoint and expand it until it encompasses your whole being.

After activating your own inner Light, activate within every soul who crosses your threshold the inner Light. Pass it as a candle, as a torch, to others.

Make your work stand the test of time by putting the Light in it. Picture your every footstep as leaving streams of light.

3. The Light Absolute

Act as a power within the inner Light. Walk and move and have your being in that Light Absolute.

Dwell on the meaning of "infusion," "correlation," "assimilation," "infiltration," and "ingestion" of that Light and Power. Be conscious of it every moment.

Give to others the degree of light they are able to accept, but do not linger in the shadow of those who attempt to take you into their struggle.

Always be in delight, joy, happiness.

4. Spiritual Energy

Realize that energy is available at all times, but that it never imposes itself on you; it must be requested.

Develop methods whereby it may be commanded.

Apply those methods.

Suggested methods to be regularized:

- ■ Unification of physical, astral, mental energy through rhythmic breath control.
- ■ Rhythmic exercises and pranayama, seven cycle breath, the breath of exertion.

PART TWO. COMMUNICATION WITH OTHER DIMENSIONS

5. Interdimensional Communication

First step in preparation is to unify physical, astral, mental bodies.

Practice the Presence of God by regular contemplation.

Study the nature of subtler energies through literature that covers the various dimensions.

Set aside all prejudices, doubts, and logical explanations.

Rest in the awareness that ability to communicate is even now functional. Do not struggle with or chastise yourself because it is not coming faster.

6. Receptivity to Higher Dimensions

Begin to recognize the receptivity of your soul to impressions from high beings.

Prepare for meditation by:

- Ringing a bell three times. Cleansing yourself of all impurities before you enter meditation chamber. Ask the sun and your own Divine Light to remove all impurities from your bodies.
- Looking into a prism of purity and into your mind. Ask if the mind is clear to receive the food of God.
- When the mind is clear, writing the inspired thought upon paper.
- Entering meditation room, placing thought upon the altar as a gift to your guides, to God.

Decrystallize your fixed attitudes.

Read Alice Bailey's *Telepathy and the Etheric Vehicle.*

7. Immortality: Realize you are immortal and teach others that they are also as the gods, even to the physical level.

8. The Nature of Shambala: Daily attune to the great Shambala energy.

PART THREE. MAKING IT WORK FOR INDIVIDUAL EVOLUTION

9. Land-Water-Air

After realization of your power, mentally focus on a point where water, air, and land meet. Feel the impression of this experience.

Realize that this experience took place through focusing attention in the etheric realms, the realms of imagination, that it led to your becoming one with material substance. Energy follows thought.

Cherish the power of the mind to focus attention first on land — water — air and then move it to the object of your desire. Know that you will get what you want.

Meditate often on this concept.

10. Discipline and Order and Use of Time

Study words "orderliness" and "discipline."

Invoke patterns in your life which are self-perpetuating —

early rising, planned activity, review of activity.
Use time as a gift.
Center yourself several times a day.
Perfect the body.
Work through old conditions through prayer, energizing, healing.
Take discipline as a joy.
Contemplate, concentrate.

11. Work

View work as a positive thing, a challenge.

Take the past influence out, look at it and say, "I no longer need this negative attitude." Feel diligent in work.

Take the first impulse of the day and follow it for a productive day, going thus from one task to another.

12. The Inner Sanctuary

Go forth inward by going first outside yourself.

Put away the outer debris of life and enter the inner sanctuary. Prepare by reading holy words, dwelling on holy thoughts, and realizing the inner Sun.

Turn all attention completely to the inner place. In the absence of all things, of thoughts, is found the inner sanctuary. Follow your inner experience, as to time spent here.

13. A Safe Place in Spirit

Realize that there is no answer on the external plane. Above all else, desire the spirit. Say to yourself, "I am only God. I am only knowledge." Do not be distracted by the temptations of the world. They are all illusions.

14. Silence, Solitude, and the Great Planetary Wind Chamber

Set aside regular periods for silence and solitude.

Detach yourself from all sound and experience around you the winds of the cosmos.

Imagine a powerful funnel of light with an opening through which you walk, dropping your ordinary nature. Feel every particle of your brain filled with light. Then go about your duties.

15. Destiny and Life Design

Make a thorough inquiry into who you are and begin to create a life design; find what capacities you can draw forth. Know that you are worthwhile.

By use of imagination, make a design from this information in order that destiny may be planned — not left to "fate." Live your life with care.

16. Ultimate Individuality

Apply universal concepts to your present-day motivation, beginning with that of ultimate individuality.

Realize that you are one of the perfected units, and begin to look at the aspects of your inner and outer reality that are unique to you.

Resolve to expand and perfect these qualities in order to contribute to the greater oneness of the universe.

Study the myriad expressions of Infinity, individualized levels of consciousness, to increase your awareness of the greater being all about you.

See the connectedness of the golden thread of light, which weaves its way through every mind on Earth.

Study and relate to these universal concepts, developing a philosophy of life useful in expanding your consciousness.

Ferret out your tendency to be judgmental. Turn it into your ally and develop it into discernment.

PART FOUR. PASSING THE TORCH — MAKING IT WORK IN THE WORLD

17. Preparation for the New World Order

Decide to serve, cleanse the emotional body, be alert to needs of fellow man, pray and meditate, and contemplate the wonders of the world, ascertain the place for service, and realize dominion over your physical world.

Maintain your integrity at all levels of being by:

- Evaluating what you consider to be your personal integrity.
- Seeking counsel, if necessary, on your role.

18. Responsibility of the Individual in Prevailing World Conditions

Pray without ceasing. Prayer is a process of awareness in the midst of activity.

Develop compassion in all situations.

Gather together individuals of like mind into a unit of power, to work invisibly.

THE WAY OF THE AVATAR

Discover the way of the avatar. Is it your way?

STILLPOINT PUBLISHING

Books that explore the expanding frontiers of human consciousness and invite fresh thinking about the nature of mankind

*For a free catalog, write to
Stillpoint Publishing
Box 640 Walpole, NH 03608
USA*